SAINTS OF THE JUBILEE

Edited by

Tim Drake

ISBN: 1-4033-1009-2 (Paperback)
ISBN: 1-4033-1008-4 (e-book)

This book is printed on acid free paper.

Cover artwork of *The Chinese Martyrs* is by Professor Li Chien-Yi.
Reprinted with permission from Li Chien-Yi and VMA Venture
Marketing Associate. All rights reserved.

Professor Li Chien-Yi teaches at the National Taiwan University of Art
and Fu-Jen Catholic University.

Cover design by Ted Schluenderfritz, Schluenderfritz Design.

1stBooks - rev. 06/19/02

Dedication

To Pope John Paul II, for having the wisdom to beatify and canonize so many Christian faithful during his pontificate.

Acknowledgements

I am most indebted to my wife, Mary. Her work in the home makes my work, and this book, possible. Her keen editorial eye caught things mine did not.

I am most grateful to each of the contributors who have worked so diligently, and for so little earthly reward, to compile the stories herein. Without you, this book would not exist.

I continue to thank the Sisters of the St. Clare Monastery in Sauk Rapids, Minnesota for their prayers on behalf of my writing. Without their prayers, and the grace of God, I could not do what I do.

I also want to thank Ted Schluenderfritz for his always creative and inspiring design work.

Contents

Foreword

Heroic Witnesses

Nothing is more foreign to contemporary culture than the very idea of a saint. The world will occasionally acknowledge the humanitarian services of a figure such as Mother Teresa of Calcutta, but only if she is repackaged as something like a super-sized social worker first. For many of us – including, alas, many Catholics – saints exist in a mythical realm, distant in time and space, the heroes and heroines of a world long dead and gone.

Two main obstacles hinder our ability to recognize saints. First, we have a mistaken idea that Christian teaching requires everyone to follow a single, narrow path. The way to eternal life is a straight gate, as Jesus himself reminds us. But anyone who looks into the lives of the saints over twenty Christian centuries will immediately notice not their sameness, but their variety. Though all of them believe in the dogmas of the Church and strive to practice Christian charity and the standard moral virtues, something in the very nature of holiness makes present to the world a living and unpredictable spirit. There is no other way to account for the unique Christian vocations of saints as different as Francis of Assisi and Ignatius of Loyola, Theresa of Avila and Thérèse of Lisieux, among many others.

But even if we get beyond a stunted notion of who saints are, we face a second obstacle. We are quite willing to believe that certain people have done good things and lived basically admirable lives. But can we really say that their time on earth offers an example of holiness? The very idea of holiness carries with it things most of us would rather not face: that some people are better than others, that certain acts are good and others are bad, and, last but not least, that there is a final standard of truth and goodness by which we will all be measured.

Oddly, the saints themselves are the ones who are most conscious of not living up to these traditional Christian standards. When Francis of Assisi tells his followers, "Let us begin again, for as yet we have done nothing," he is not merely setting impossible goals or indulging in a dangerous perfectionism. He is more acutely aware than the rest of us – precisely because of his own spiritual progress – how far we are from anything that might be called true holiness.

And that is only one of many reasons why the lives of the saints are an important and neglected resource in our world. We can look to the saints as examples of how a truly Christian life can be lived in a variety of circumstances. All sorts of controversies exist about theological, philosophical, and social questions. And the lives of the saints inevitably get drawn into these controversies. But saints – as these are certified by the authority of the Church – give us a kind of touchstone over and above all controversies. And remind us that holiness manages to take new and unforeseen forms in order to deal with the many problems in which we are embroiled.

The modern saints, which have been a special interest of Pope John Paul II's, are especially helpful in this. Strictly speaking, we do not merely imitate saints the way we might imitate a well-known teacher or artist or public figure. The Church has always taught that we are *in communion* with the saints in the Body of Christ, which is the Church itself spread out through the ages. We still participate in the faith of Peter and Paul, Martha and Mary, and all the saints and martyrs. But there is no denying that the modern saints have special relevance to us because they frequently deal with problems quite close to those we encounter every day.

The present volume usefully selects a variety of modern saints canonized during the Jubilee. It could easily be much longer. But the figures treated here are representative of the many kinds of heroic witnesses that the faith still produces and the kinds of problems and opposition they face. People who have received special revelations, such as the three children of Fatima or Saint Faustina Kowalska, correspond most closely to what many expect saints to be. Though all of them were from quite humble backgrounds, they were given special communications that no one could have anticipated. The children at Fatima – still a tiny, out-of-the-way village almost a century after their visions – were entrusted with messages that seem much too large for the recipients. What could these very young peasant children have known, for instance, about the coming persecutions in Russia, which were revealed to them before the Communist Revolution had even occurred? Or how could a poor, barely educated Polish woman have conceived of a new devotion to the Divine Mercy and made it current against all human odds? The answer probably lies in the fact that like a poor carpenter's son from an out-of-the-way village in Northern Palestine, the power of what they had to say has little to do with power as the world judges things.

But such special revelations are rare. Some saints, particularly the martyrs, remind us of the more typical need for heroic virtue in our time and the violent reaction to the encounter with the Good News that has occurred since the origins of Christianity. The Chinese martyrs described here, for instance, were the victims of various waves of repression. Often these deaths are excused today, even within Christian circles, as resulting from the Church's participation in Western imperialism. Sometimes Christians did identify themselves too closely with Western cultures as they went out to preach the Gospel, and Pope John Paul II has apologized for those abuses.

But as many of the examples collected here illustrate, missionaries have also been a courageous force of liberation where local governments attempted to keep their peoples in political and intellectual bondage.

We see this most clearly in the present volume in the Martyrs of Nowogrodek, simple missionaries of mercy in a non-Catholic area of Eastern Europe raked by the twin scourges of Nazism and Communism. These nuns did not convert the local population but won them over by their good-natured assistance to all who needed it, including their prayers to suffer in place of the Christians and Jews with families who were the targets of Nazi Germany's murderous racial theories. Their prayers were answered; they ended up in a common mass grave, murdered for no reason other than they offered a different vision than the one that arrived by military conquest.

A similar case worked itself out in Mexico at the beginning of the twentieth century where a revolutionary regime claiming to want to improve the lives of ordinary Mexican people believed it could only do so by persecuting the Church that almost all Mexicans belonged to – and have heroically adhered to to this day. Mexico's continuing enthusiasm for the faith probably owes no small debt to the many witnesses who died so that their fellow Mexicans could live as Christians.

There are examples of more immediate relevance to our own situation here as well. Saint Katharine Drexel is a case that all of us living amid the wealth of the United States must take to heart. The daughter of a highly successful father and heroically charitable step-mother, she had to figure out what to do with the great material blessings God had provided to her family. She did not indulge in the mistaken belief that wealth per se is evil. Instead, she rightly regarded her inheritance as entailing special responsibilities. The schools and other welfare institutions that she founded – for the poor and for Black and Native Americans – struggled against deep-seated social prejudice. But in the end they resulted in a concrete offering of God's love to many who had been excluded from America's blessings.

There are other lessons here. For example, as medical technology becomes more powerful, it also becomes more distant from the human needs of the sick. Medical schools have tried to overcome this problem by training doctors to be more sensitive to the personal dimension of treating the sick and their families. But this is essentially a side issue for what, in its essence, is technical training. A figure such as Saint Maria Josefa, foundress of the Servants of Jesus, provides an important corrective for those medical professionals who claim to believe. She trained the nuns of her order to deal with the sick: "Always see the person of Jesus Christ in the patient." You can call this a pious aspiration, or, if you are a believer in God and real sanctity, you can call this the most realistic way of dealing with human suffering. Sister Maria Josefa also understood another important truth often overlooked in our technologized approach to medicine: ultimately, we all die, and the most important thing for the sick and for those who care for them is sanctification through the right attitude and action in the midst of illness. Not only did she succeed in this religious task, she was highly effective as an administrator (93 religious houses all over the world exist today thanks to her vision and efforts) – and with a humility and concern for others that is often absent among those engaged in great humanitarian and spiritual undertakings.

Anyone who feels that modern life offers us few opportunities for the kind of holiness we associate with earlier ages will find a counter argument presented here. God's love and inspiration are never lacking in any age. We have the saints to prove it. It is up to those of us who say we believe this to follow these saints in making our own faith a living reality.

Robert Royal

Robert Royal is president of the Faith & Reason Institute, Washington, D.C. His book, The Catholic Martyrs of the Twentieth Century: A Comprehensive World History *was published by Crossroad for the Jubilee Year.*

Introduction

A Time for Saints

Growing up as a Lutheran, saints were not something familiar to me. They were not something we spoke about, and they certainly were not individuals whose intercession we depended upon. We were, as you might say, saintless.

A casual teenage encounter with St. Joseph, at my friend's home, changed all that. Sitting atop my friend's dresser sat a prayer card featuring St. Joseph. Not only had I never seen such a beautifully painted depiction of Christ's foster-father, but I also had never read a prayer like the one contained on the backside of that card. The prayer was as beautiful as the artwork on the front, and called to mind Joseph's very human fatherhood.

That card was the first step in what would be my long journey toward the Catholic Church and my understanding of the richness of the living Church – the Saints. In learning about the saints, I discovered an entire sister and brotherhood that seemed to have been abandoned by my Lutheran tradition. That is a tragic loss.

As I write this, the Congregation for the Causes of Saints is preparing for the canonization of three very notable saints in the year 2002 – Juan Diego, a Mexican visionary; Josemaria Escriva; the founder of Opus Dei; and Padre Pio, an Italian priest and mystic. I continue to marvel at the inspiring models of faith that the Church offers up for us in our own struggles to lead faithful lives.

The year 2000, in addition to being the Jubilee year, proved to be a record-breaking year for saints in the record-breaking pontificate of Pope John Paul II. Canonization ceremonies during the Jubilee year added 151 new saints to the Church's calendar – thereby declaring more saints than in any other year during Pope John Paul II's reign. In addition, the pope beatified 56 men, women, and children during the year.

This is nothing unusual for the Pope. In fact, as of this writing, during his 23-year pontificate Pope John Paul has canonized 456 saints and beatified 1,282.

We might ask ourselves why the Holy Father is doing this? Some have criticized him for the canonizations, describing him as a "saint machine."

Yet Pope John Paul seems to recognize something that many others do not, or if they do, it is something that they have forgotten. Having lived through World War II, the Holy Father knows that the 20th century was one of the bloodiest history has ever seen. A great many of the Church's newest saints come from this time period, and the majority of them were martyrs for their faith. Pope John Paul also recognizes that the faithful will need these additional role models as we progress through the 21st century.

Saints, it might be said, are ordinary people who have lived extraordinary lives. In many ways, they are similar to us. They are our neighbors, our family, and our friends. Yet, they are also very different. They provide a shining example for us of lives lived, and sometimes given, in devotion to God. They are examples of people striving for holiness. They are signs of contradiction.

This book is not meant to be a complete survey of the Jubilee's 151 new saints and 56 newly blesseds. Rather, it is a snapshot. It provides the stories of a variety of modern saintly examples from Asia, Europe, and North and South America as a way of introducing these new saints. They include men and women, lay people and religious, children and adults. They include the stories of popular saints, such as Katharine Drexel, Francisco and Jacinta Marto, and Sister Faustina Kowalska, as well as stories of those perhaps not so familiar – Andrew the Catechist, Augustine Tchao and the Chinese Martyrs, Maria Josefa, and the inspirational martyrs of Nowogrodek.

May their lives continue to provide an example of holiness to those of us called to live our faith in the 21st century. May they urge us forward in our own efforts to spread our faith in the New Evangelization before us.

Tim Drake
Saint Cloud, Minnesota
February 8, 2002 – Feast of St. Jerome Emiliani

Beatifications

Tim Drake

A Saintly Sacrifice:
The Martyrs of Nowogrodek

By Kathryn Lively

When Frances Siedliska, known during her religious life as Mother Mary of Jesus the Good Shepherd, founded the Congregation of the Sisters of the Holy Family of Nazereth in 1875, it was her intent that this order be a model for complete selflessness and spiritual devotion. Willing to distance herself from the worldly decadence and wealth that characterized the Polish nobility into which she was born, Mother Mary sought in her contemplative life to serve and console others, particularly families, with the same compassion and humility she believed Mary, Joseph, and young Jesus possessed.

To say that Mother Mary's example had little or no effect on her homeland or the rest of the world would be a falsehood, particularly when one considers the rapid growth of the order since its founding. Twenty-nine foundations had been established around the world at the time of Mother Mary's death in 1902, each adhering to their foundress's call to give totally of oneself and dedicate one's deeds to Christ's Church. Nowhere will one find a more inspirational example of such sacrifice than with the story of the courageous martyrs from the Holy Family of Nazareth convent in Nowogrodek during the Nazi invasion of World War II.

In August, 1929, Nowogrodek was but a small village located near the larger town of Grodno in what was then the northeast region of Poland (the area, following World War II, became property of the USSR and is today, with the fall of Communism in Eastern Europe, known as Belarus.) There, at the behest of Bishop Zygmunt Lozinski, Sister Maria Stella Mardosiewicz and one other fellow nun from the Congregation of the Sister of the Holy Family of Nazareth arrived to establish a convent and school, a task that proved in the beginning to be quite arduous.

As Nowogrodek was populated primarily by Protestant and Jewish peoples, a natural suspicion of these strange women — easily noticeable in their flowing black habits and veils — spread throughout the town. This suspicion presented the new convent's superior Sister Stella and her charges, who would eventually number eleven, with an uncomfortable atmosphere. Complaints, however, were seldom, despite beginning their new ministry in the midst of indifference and scorn in a hovel of a home where the kitchen and bedroom were one.

3

Bishop Lozinski, a native of Nowogrodek, offered unconditional support and blessings, telling the nuns how the town would soon come to view their presence not with stubborn disdain but with great joy, and how one day their existence would be a source of local pride. The nuns, bolstered by this esteem, accepted the challenge, holding fast to their faith in Christ and to foundress Mother Mary's example of serving the community families with love. To take a line from Shakespeare, the nun's "killed" Nowogrodek with kindness, smiling graciously in the direction of stern faces and turned backs, always offering a kind word and a silent prayer.

Whether by the grace of God or by admiration of the nuns' perseverance, it would come to pass that the townspeople succumbed to the charms of the women in black. The twelve were now so much a fixture in the community that great concern often arose among townspeople when they all did not appear publicly together when performing their various acts of charity.

An affectionate moniker, *the prie-dieux*, or "the kneelers," was bestowed upon them, as the nuns could often be found in the local Church of the Transfiguration kneeling at the left side of the Altar in prayer. To watch the sisters ascend the steep hill to get to the church was an equally awe-inspiring sight, as Maria Starzynska wrote in 1992, "it seemed as though they were gliding along, almost as if they were flying up the hill like birds. Perhaps their wide habits, their pleated collars, and their windblown veils made them look so picturesque."

It was this growing camaraderie between the nuns and the townspeople that provided a much-needed spiritual balm on that fateful day, September 1, 1939, when Adolf Hitler's troops invaded Poland. Though Nowogrodek, as with the rest of Poland and Germany, had been living tenuously for years under the shadow of the rising Nazi empire, this attack made all too immediate the prospect of danger for the small town. Even though the Germans were on the extreme other side of the country, their efforts were certainly not a topic at which to scoff.

Sixteen days later, Russian troops marched through the eastern border of Poland and occupied the land, leaving the nuns of the Holy Family of Nazareth with no recourse but to pray for themselves and their community. The war had officially and literally entered their backyard, and the Russians, steeped heavily in their godless Communistic beliefs, saw no need for any of the quaint Catholic trappings or people of Nowogrodek.

The nuns, forced to close the convent and school, surrendered their habits and dressed in secular clothing, were transformed immediately into paupers, begging in the streets for food and shelter and relying on local acts of generosity. To this end, the sisters saw no other choice but to separate, reuniting whenever they were fortunate enough to celebrate Mass with the local pastor, Father Aleksander Zienkiewicz. These moments, however, were rare and likely clandestine.

Where Communism strove to destroy their faith through confiscation, the nuns continued to persevere with prayer and faith in Christ, thereby proving that a convent need not be enclosed by walls to have spiritual direction. Sister Stella and the other eleven nuns continued the charitable acts that characterized their order by lending support to those hit hardest by the Russian occupation, making every place where they were able to live their convent.

For two years the Nowogrodek nuns survived in this manner, throughout the Nazi takeover of the town and country. By June of 1941, Nowogrodek existed under the Nazi flag. The nuns, though hardly esteemed by their Nazi captors, were granted permission to return to the convent to live and to attend Mass. Others in Nowogrodek were not as fortunate to be treated as such.

For the next two years the Nazi troops celebrated their occupation of Nowogrodek by rounding up as many Jews and Communist sympathizers they could expose and executing them in public. As during the Communist occupation, the Sisters of the Holy Family of Nazareth combated this latest, bloodier siege the only way they could: through steadfast prayer. Now they would add the names of the many souls whose lives were lost needlessly, murdered solely because of their heritage and faith.

By late July of 1943, not even the constant prayer and attention of the nuns to the suffering families of Nowogrodek could soothe the emotional and physical pain brought on by the war. The slaughter of the Jewish people was as commonplace as buying a loaf of bread, and it seemed that the Gestapo would not rest until every trace of the Jews was obliterated. Sister Stella and her companions, having raised the ire of the Gestapo through their acts of mercy and unwavering faith in Christ, intensified their prayers when approximately 120 area factory workers, many of them heads of households, were arrested and awaited execution.

"Oh, God, if sacrifice of life is needed, accept it from us who are free from family obligations. Spare those who have wives and children," prayed Sister Stella. Her companions prayed in kind, all willing to give their own lives to spare those of the arrested. One can only imagine the reactions of the nuns when a Nazi civilian confronted them on the night of July 31, 1943 and ordered them to report to the office of the Kommissar, offering no reason for the summons.

Sister Maria Malgorzata Banas, the oldest of the twelve, was selected to remain behind in the convent with Father Zienkiewicz in the event neither Sister Stella nor any of the other nuns returned. The purpose of the summons was debatable – arrest, the dissolution of the convent, expulsion from the town – and though a sense of dread permeated the convent, the nuns nonetheless ventured toward their destiny with high hearts, confident in the Lord's Will.

Sister Stella's pleas to grant their offer of sacrifice were heard in the early hours of August 1, 1943, when the eleven nuns of the Holy Family of Nazareth were arrested in the place of the 120 workers. From the Kommissar's office they were herded into a van and transported to a remote spot in the woods bordering Nowogrodek, where an open grave large enough to hold their bodies awaited them. There, kneeling side by side in the habits of their order, the sisters bade each other farewell, hoping to meet again with Christ in Heaven. One by one, beginning with Sister Stella, the nuns were shot, their lifeless bodies tumbling into the grave.

The Sisters of the Holy Family of Nazareth who willingly and unselfishly gave their lives so that others might live:

- Sister Maria Stella Mardosewicz, born 1888
- Sister Mary Imelda Zak, born 1892
- Sister Mary Rajmunda Kukulowicz, born 1892
- Sister Maria Daniela Juzwik, born 1895
- Sister Maria Kanuta Chrobot, born 1896
- Sister Maria Gwidona Cierpka, born 1900
- Sister Maria Sergia Rapieg, born 1900
- Sister Maria Kanizja Mackiewicz, born 1904
- Sister Maria Felicyta Borowik, born 1905
- Sister Maria Heliodora Matustzewska, born 1906
- Sister Maria Boromea Narmuntowicz, born 1916

In response to the Sisters' offering of life, the plans for the arrested workers were changed. They were deported to work camps in Germany, and some were even released, including rector Father Zienkiewicz.

Fearing the worst when, after several days, the nuns did not return, Sister Malgorzata and Father Zienkiewicz went into hiding and managed to elude the clutches of the Gestapo. Dressed in secular clothing, Sister Malgorzata waited out the weeks following the execution of her companions before risking a solo journey through the woods in search of their remains. She would tend to the mass grave and pray for the souls of her beloved sisters until the war ended.

With the end of the war brought a change to Poland. Nowogrodek was once again the property of Communist Russia. People were being evicted from their homes, plans for developing the area were being made, and all the while the martyr nuns of Nowogrodek lay in the ground in the woods. Were it not for Sister Malgorzata's loyalty to her order and to her slain sisters in caring for their grave, it is likely that this magnanimous sacrifice made by Sister Stella and her companions might never be known. Their bodies were exhumed in March of 1945 and laid to rest on the grounds of the Church of the Transfiguration following a Mass of Christian Burial.

In the decades following the end of World War II, interest in Catholic martyrs in the European Theater became more evident and obvious. By the mid 1980s the world was already aware of two prominent Catholic figures – Maximilian Kolbe, canonized in 1982, and Edith Stein, beatified in 1987 and eventually canonized in 1999. No doubt the curiosity to learn more about those who died in the wake of Nazi terror for the sake of their Savior grew in this time, when those who survived the war and the concentration camps continued to heal, emotionally and physically.

In 1991, the cause for the canonization of Sister Stella, superior of the Nowogrodek Congregation of the Sisters of the Holy Family of Nazareth, and her ten companions was officially opened. Citing the nuns' fidelity to their perpetual vows and the rule of their order, as set by Mother Mary Frances Siedliska (who was beatified on April 23, 1989), it was the hope of those initiating the process that the nuns would be recognized as true martyrs of the Catholic Faith. Just as the heroic virtues of St. Maximilian Kolbe, who sacrificed his life so that another man could live and be with his family, were acknowledged, so those in the order of the Holy Family of Nazareth hoped the same honor would be granted to their fallen sisters.

Nearly a decade later, it appeared as if Bishop Lozinski's words of encouragement, spoken more than half a century before when the nuns of Nowogrodek faced a lesser crisis, were prophetic. It was true that at the time of the Russian and Nazi occupations that the nuns were often a symbol of hope and peace for the townspeople. This opinion of the nuns endured over the years and was confirmed with the words of Father Yaroslaw Hrynaszkiewicz of Grodno, Belarus when relating the news of their pending beatification: "All the faithful are aware and feel happy." Hrynaszkiewicz brought this regional pride with him and over 150 Belorusians to the Basilica of St. Peter's on March 5, 2000 when Pope John Paul II beatified Sister Stella, her ten companions, and 33 other venerable martyrs of the faith.

"These martyrs made their lives a generous response to God's gift and are eloquent models of Christian witness for us all," the pontiff declared. He addressed a multitude of the faithful, many of whom had traveled from as far away as Mexico and Vietnam to witness the beatification of martyrs from their homelands. With regards to the Nowogrodek martyrs, the Pope offered a brief yet powerful testimonial.

"Jesus' words come to mind: 'There is no greater love than this: to lay down one's life for one's friend.' (cf. Jn 15:13). They perfectly confirmed the truth of these words by their lives filled with devotion and by their death," he said. "Before the war and during the occupation, they zealously served the inhabitants of Nowogrodek, participating actively in pastoral care and education and engaging in various works of charity. Their love for those among whom they fulfilled their mission took on special significance during the hours of the Nazi invasion."

These nuns of Nowogrodek, these eleven prie-dieux, were among the first Catholic martyrs to be beatified in the Jubilee Year. It is only fitting that a pontiff from their homeland, one who risked the wrath of the Nazis by secretly studying for the priesthood, could bestow this honor upon them and help to perpetuate the memory of their saintly sacrifice.

Kathryn Lively's first novel, Little Flowers, was published in 2001 by Highbridge Press. Currently she is finishing a mystery novel. In her spare time she edits the monthly newsletter of the Catholic Writers Association, "The Write Stuff," and maintains the group's web site. For more information on her writing,visit her web site at http://www.livelywriter.com.

Andrew the Catechist

By Kathryn Mulderink

In Vietnam, Christianity's vibrancy is rooted in the labors and fidelity of generations of catechists who continued to serve Christ and the Gospel for centuries, long after foreign missionaries had been expelled and native clergy prohibited from exercising their ministry. Among the 44 martyrs declared "blessed" by Pope John Paul II during the very first beatification of the Jubilee Year 2000 was Andrew the Catechist of Vietnam. Though he preached for only a few years, his witness of faith was so strong that he has been remembered by millions of Vietnamese faithful for more than 350 years.

The story of seventeenth century Christianity in Cocicina, Vietnam, and of Andrew's place in it, was told by Jesuit missionary Father Alexander de Rhodes, who was for Vietnam what Matteo Ricci was for China, compiling the first dictionary of the national language and developing the written characters still used today. He was an eyewitness to the imprisonment, condemnation to death, and martyrdom of Andrew, and wrote down the first account five years later.

Son of a devoutly Christian mother, Andrew was born in 1625 in Ran Ran, Vietnam. He was the youngest son, and had a rather weak constitution but he exhibited a keen mind, sound judgement, and a soul that tended towards goodness. At the insistence of Andrew's mother, Fr. de Rhodes accepted him among his students, and he applied himself to the study of Chinese characters to such a degree that he soon surpassed his fellow students.

He received baptism along with his mother, only three years before his death, at the age of 19 or 20. One year later, he became a Catechist, and in 1643, along with other catechists, he made a vow to serve the Church for the rest of his life.

When the king of Annam (Vietnam's ancient name) ordered a halt to the spread of Christianity in his kingdom, the natives were forbidden to join the "new" religion. In late July 1644, the Mandarin Ong Nghè Bo had come back to the province carrying with him the order to halt the expansion of Christianity, and decided to act immediately and aggressively against the Vietnamese catechists. On the evening of July 25, 1644, soldiers were sent to Fr. de Rhodes' house with orders to pick up a catechist named Ignatius, but when he was not there, they broke into the priest's residence. Finding young Andrew, they beat him, bound him, and brought him to the Mandarin explaining that he was a catechist just like Ignatius, since "he had always spoken of the law of Christ to everyone in the village, exhorting them to receive it." Detained, Andrew was counseled to "give up his idiotic opinion," and to renounce his faith. The intrepid catechist responded that he was a Christian, and was willing to suffer anything, rather than "abandon the law he professed." Urging them to prepare any torture, he firmly stated that for his beliefs he would willingly embrace "both the suffering and the most glorious death." He was condemned to death.

The following day, Fr. Rhodes and some Portuguese merchants arrived at the house where Andrew was being held and found him serene and happy to be able to suffer for Christ. With tears in their eyes, they offered him their prayers, and Andrew asked them to pray for themselves too, that God might grant them the grace to remain faithful to him and to the "infinite love of the Lord who gave his own life for mankind." He repeated these thoughts and then concluded, saying, "Let us give love for love to our God, let us give life for life."

In the afternoon of July 26, 1644, thirty soldiers arrived and ordered him to follow them to the place he would be executed. Andrew thanked the Lord that the hour of his sacrifice had arrived, and bid farewell to those with him in prison. Fr. de Rhodes, following the customs of the land, asked for and received permission to spread a mat out under the body of Andrew to catch his blood, but Andrew refused, preferring that his blood fall to the ground, in imitation of Christ. Fr. de Rhodes knelt beside him.

Andrew continued to encourage the Christians present to remain firm in their faith, not to be saddened on account of his death, and to help him with their prayers to be faithful to the end. Spears pierced the left side of his body, and when a soldier brandished a scimitar to decapitate him, he exclaimed in a loud voice, "Jesus!" bearing witness to his Christian faith and love.

Fr. De Rhodes retrieved the body, which was shipped to Macao for burial. When pirates attacked the transport ship, it struck a rock, and a hole was torn in the hull. Miraculously, a large stone rolled into the gap, holding out the water, and the ship was able to deliver its cargo.

Despite the passing of centuries, Vietnamese Catholics have never forgotten this young catechist, whom they consider to be the first martyr of their country, and a powerful intercessor for their fidelity to the faith.

Kathryn Mulderink, OCDS, BA, lives with her husband and seven children on 10 acres of the orchard belt in Michigan. After studying to be a teacher, she became active in family and educational issues, was invited to become a board member of the Michigan Parent Action Group, and edited the organization's newsletter. She was a charter member of the Michigan Catholic Home-Educators and the first editor of its newsletter, Opus Gloriae. She is a certified Marian Catechist, a member of the Marian Catechists Writer's Association, and a member of the Catholic Writer's Association. She currently freelances between diapers and homeschool lessons.

Tim Drake

Viva Cristo Rey! - 25 Mexican Martyr Saints
Blessed Cristobal Magallanes and Companions

By Ann Ball

Twenty five Mexican martyrs were canonized by Pope John Paul II on May 21, 2000. Twenty two of these were diocesan priests; three were lay men. They were killed in hatred of the faith during the turbulent years from 1915 to 1937.

Many North Americans are largely unaware of the persecution of the Catholic Church during the 1920's and 1930's in Mexico. The bitter conflict known as the Cristero Rebellion (the Cristiada) has rarely been mentioned by historians.

Under the dictatorship of Plutarco Elias Calles (1924-1928) the Mexican government was bitterly anti-clerical. Calles wanted to eradicate the Catholic Church.. In 1925 he expelled foreign clergy from the country and confiscated the property of church-run schools, hospitals and other charitable works. In 1926, 33 articles against the church which became known as the "Ley Calles" [Calles Law] were passed.

After notifying Pope Pius XI, the bishops closed the churches in protest. A petition to the government containing over two million signatures was ignored and eventually, in 1927, some of the faithful took up arms to defend religious liberty.

With the enactment of the anti-Catholic laws, the church in Mexico was driven underground. With an almost supernatural stubbornness, many of the Mexican clergy determined to remain with the souls entrusted to their care, sharing their sorrows and working to alleviate their sufferings. They offered the Holy Sacrifice in various locations and comforted and strengthened the people with the Sacraments, given in hiding. In order to serve their flocks, the priests risked imprisonment, torture and execution.

A majority of the Catholic Bishops of Mexico opposed armed conflict and worked from exile to reach agreement with the government. Other key players for detante were from the United States. At last, an agreement known as "the arreglos" [arrangement] was reached in 1929 under Mexican President Emilio Portes Gil. On June 27 the churches were re-opened. Some conflicts continued throughout the 1930's, and the Mexican Catholics' battle cry - "Viva Cristo Rey" - resounds today in the lives and heroism of its glorious martyr saints.

Six of these martyrs, Fathers Batiz, Correa, Robles, de la Mora, Aguilar, and Maldonado, were members of the Knights of Columbus and as such were the first Knights to be canonized. It is believed that Salvador Lara was also a Knight although no records can be found to confirm his membership. By 1923 there were nearly 6,000 Knights in Mexico, but the Mexican government outlawed the group and banned distribution of their publications. The Knights of the United States did much to make Americans aware of the persecutions south of the border.

Father Cristobal Magallanes and Father Agustin Caloca

Father Cristobal Magallanes had carefully studied Pope Leo XIII's ideas of social justice, and he attempted to put them into practice. He established catechetical centers, and schools in his villages, built a dam for water and set up small land developments for the poor. He began a magazine called *El Rosario* (The Rosary) to teach his people. On May 21, 1927, fighting broke out between the federal forces under General Goni and the Cristeros in the area. Father Magallanes was on his way to a rancho to celebrate Mass when he was captured and taken back to Totatiche, where he was the parish priest. He was jailed next to his curate, Father Caloca, in the Colotitlan municipal palace.

Father Agustin Caloca was in the seminary in Guadalajara when it was closed, but he continued his studies under Father Magallanes and was ordained in 1923. He was assigned as curate at Totalice, and was also the prefect of the seminary. When the government troops were approaching, he ordered the seminarians to disperse. He was attempting to go into hiding when he was captured.

The government troops accused Father Magallanes of promoting the Cristero movement in the region. In defense, he showed them a copy of *El Rosario* where he had written: "Religion is not propagated nor conserved by means of arms. Neither Jesus Christ, nor his apostles, nor the Church has to employ violence to accomplish their ends. The weapons of the church are to convince and to persuade by means of the Word."

While awaiting execution, Father Magallanes told Father Caloca, "Cheer up, God loves the martyrs... one moment and we are in Heaven." Father Caloca, understood, and added, "We have lived for God and in Him we die."

Before he was shot, Father Magallanes distributed his few possessions among the soldiers ordered to shoot him, and gave them absolution. He asked permission to speak and said, "I am innocent and I die innocent. I forgive with all my heart those responsible for my death, and I ask God that the shedding of my blood serves toward the peace of our divided Mexico."

About midday on May 25, 1927, the priests were shot by a firing squad in front of an adobe wall behind the municipal building at Colotitlan, Jalisco. In 1933 when Father Caloca's remains were translated to Totalice, his heart was found to be entire and incorrupt with a piece of a bullet still in it.

Father David Galvan

Although David Galvan had completed the preparatory course at the seminary of Guadalajara with good grades, he left to work for three years. He began to live a wild lifestyle and in one episode he was jailed for hitting his girlfriend in a drunken rage. David seemed to feel God calling him, and he changed radically, putting away his affection for worldly things and supporting difficult and adverse circumstances with patience and tranquillity. After a year of stringent probation, he was allowed to return to the seminary, and he was ordained in 1909. He became a teacher at the seminary.

During the carranzista revolution, he was arrested for being a priest, but was eventually released. There were often skirmishes in the area, and in mid-January of 1915, during one of these, Father Galvan spent more than six hours in the line of fire, helping the fallen soldiers.

On January 30, there was another confrontation in downtown Guadalajara between the villistas and the carranzistas. The streets of the city were covered with wounded and dead. When Father Galvan prepared to go to their aid, one of his friends told him he might be killed. He answered, "And if I am killed? What greater glory is there than to die saving a soul?"

He went to look for another priest to help him. The first one he asked excused himself, saying he wasn't a pastor. Father Galvan said, "I am not going because of obligation, but because of charity." Father Jose Araiza offered to go with him, and they left to assist the fallen. On the way into town, they were arrested by soldiers and taken before Lt. Col. Vera at the Civil Hospital, of Guadalajara who ordered their execution. Father Galvan was shot, but Father Araiza was later ransomed and released.

Father Luis Batiz, David Roldan, Salvador Lara, Manuel Moralez

The four martyrs of Zacatecas were killed under the pretense that they were trying to rouse the town against the government. The National League for the Defense of Religious Liberty (LNDLR) was founded in Chalchihuites with the aim of defending, by peaceful and legal means, the rights of the Catholic Church. July 29, there was a meeting attended by about 600 people. At the meeting, the president of the league, Manuel Moralez, said, "The League will be peaceful, without mixing in political affairs. Our project is to plead with the government to order the repeal of the constitutional articles that oppress religious liberty." When these martyrs were arrested, the townspeople were told that they would be taken to the capital to make statements. Instead, without formal or legal judicial means, they were shot a little distance from town.

Father Louis Batiz was the spiritual director of the seminary at Durango, and the parish priest of Chalchihuites. A zealous pastor, he created a workshop for Catholic workers and established a parish school. At night, he taught catechism to both children and adults. In 1925, he cautioned his parishioners that the closing of the churches was not done by the government and that Catholics should not take up arms but must conduct themselves in a Christian manner. After the meeting of the National League, he was accused of plotting an uprising and a group of soldiers arrested him in the home where he was staying.

David Roldan was born in Chalchihuites in 1907. He entered the seminary, but had to leave because of family finances. An orderly and responsible young man, he often helped Father Batiz with his pastoral duties. A mineworker, he was held in high esteem by his supervisors and his co-workers. David was a member of A.C.J.M. (the youth of Catholic Action) and was Vice President of the National League. He worked hard gathering signatures on a petition to overturn the oppressive anti-religious laws.

Salvador Lara also attended the seminary in Durango, and he, too, had to drop out and go to work because of his family's poor finances. He helped Father Batiz with his parish work, was president of Catholic Action, and secretary of the League. When Father Batiz was arrested, Lara called a meeting to see how to free the priest by legal means. A group of soldiers broke into the meeting at Salvador's home and called out the names of the officers of the League. They were taken to the municipal offices where Father Batiz was being held.

Manuel Morales, president of the League, was also a former seminarian who had to leave to help support his family. He married and had three children. An exemplary husband and father, he was the secretary of the circle of Catholic Workers and a member of Catholic Action. He was arrested with Lara and Roldan.

At about noon on August 15, 1926, the four were put into two cars that left on the road to Zacatecas. In the mountains near Puerto Santa Teresa, the cars pulled over and the prisoners were taken out. They were offered freedom if they recognized Calles's anti-religious laws. All four refused. Father Batiz and Manuel were led forward. Father Batiz asked the soldiers to free Manuel Morales because he had children to support, but Manuel told them, "I am dying for God, and God will care for my children." Then he raised his hat, and the soldiers fired, killing both. The two youths were brought forward then and, facing their executioners, each cried out, "Long live Christ the King and the Virgin of Guadalupe!" Salvador's cry was so loud that it unnerved the executioners, and he had to be given the coup de grace. His youth and heroism impressed one of the soldiers who said, "What a pity we had to kill this man so grand and strong.

Father Jenaro Sanchez

Father Jenaro Sanchez was pastor at Tecolotlan, Jalisco. During the persecution, he continued exercising his ministry as well as he could. He seemed afraid of little. He told a friend, "I think in this persecution many will be killed and I believe I will be one of the first."

On January 17, 1927, Father Sanchez was in the countryside with some villagers when a group of soldiers began following them. He was arrested and taken back to Tecolotlan. Near midnight, he was led out to a place called La Loma where there was a large mesquite tree. A man living nearby testified as to what happened next.

The soldiers put a rope around the priest's neck. He said, "Good, my countrymen, you are going to hang me. But I pardon you, and my Father God also pardons you and long live Christ the King!"

After the execution, one of the soldiers went to the house and told the man who later testified, "We are putting you in charge of the man who is hanging there. If anyone cuts him down, we will hang you, too!"

After the soldiers left, the man went to look at the body of the priest and realized it had been shot and stabbed with a bayonet. Because the body was so badly disfigured it remained where it was for some time before anyone recognized who it was. When identified as the parish priest, the body was taken to the cemetery and buried.

Father Mateo Correa

After attending the seminary of Zacatecas on a scholarship, Father Mateo Correa was assigned as parish priest of Concepcion de Oro. Here he became a close friend of the Pro-Juarez family. He baptized Humberto Pro, and gave First Communion to Miguel Pro, both of whom were later killed in hatred of the Faith. Miguel, a Jesuit, was the first Mexican martyr to be Beatified, in 1988.

Father Correa was sent to Colotlan and after 1910, because of the persecution, he stayed in hiding for a time at Leon until things calmed down. In 1926 he was assigned to Valparaiso. One day, the now elderly Father Correa was taking Viaticum to a sick person when he was surprised by a group of soldiers, and was taken to the military commander where he was accused of being in league with the Cristeros. He was taken to Durango and ordered to hear the confessions of some of the Cristeros who were in jail, awaiting execution. Father Correa prepared the young men for death, encouraging them to face the firing squad bravely. When the commander,

General Ortiz, demanded to know what they had told the priest in their confession, the brave confessor refused. The irritated general then told Father Correo that he also would be shot. "You can do that," Father Correo said, "But don't you know, general, that a priest must guard the secret of confession? I am ready to die." Father Correo was taken out of the city and shot on February 6, 1927.

Father Julio Alvarez

Father Alvarez served at Mechoacanejo, Jalisco all of his priestly life. A zealous pastor, he inculcated in his parishioners a great love for the Eucharist and for Our Lady. Indefatigable in his ministry, he continuously visited all the ranchos in the area. A man of profound prayer, his parishioners would often find him reciting his breviary in front of the Blessed Sacrament. He had a special love for the poor, going so far as to give his own clothes away to them. After the suspension of the public cult, he exercised his ministry in secret, often performing baptisms in the mountains and valleys near the town.

On March 26, 1927 Father Alvarez was going to a rancho to say Mass when he was surprised by a party of soldiers. They led him, tied to the saddle of a horse, through several cities to Leon where General Amaro sentenced him to be shot.

On March 30, about five in the morning, he was called out. Father Alvarez asked if they were going to kill him and the Captain explained that they had orders to do so. "Good," responded the priest. "I know that you have to kill me because you are ordered to do so, but only let me say a few words." The Captain acquiesced and the priest continued, "I am going to die innocent because I have done nothing wrong. My crime is to be a minister of God. I pardon you." He then crossed his arms and the soldiers received the order to fire. His body was thrown onto a trash heap near the parish church of Mechocanejo.

Father David Uribe

The pastor of Iguala, Guerrero, Father David tried to integrate Christian spirituality into all phases of his parishioners' lives. He said, "You should always try to help your parishioners see how they can intelligently unite their social life with the Christian life."

Because of the persecution, he was driven into hiding and forced to leave his people from time to time. At one time he went to Mexico City, but constantly thought of returning to his people. In one letter he wrote, "I was anointed with the oil of the saints and made a priest. Why should I not be anointed with my blood in defense of souls?"

Returning to Iguala, he was recognized, arrested, and taken by train to Cuernavaca. On the eve of his death while he was in prison, he wrote, "I declare that I am innocent of the things of which I am accused. I am in the hands of God and the Virgin of Guadalupe. I pardon all my enemies and I beg pardon from any that I have offended."

On April 11, 1927, he was removed from his cell and was apparently being taken to Mexico City. On the morning of April 12, near San Jose Vidal, he was shot in the back of the head and his body was abandoned.

Father Sabas Reyes

Sabas Reyes Salazar finished his early education and seminary in Guadalajara and was ordained in the Diocese of Taumalipus in 1911. He ministered in parishes in Guadalupe. When the persecution began, he was sent to Totolan.

In January 1927, government troops took over the parish church, converting it into a stable for the horses after breaking the images and setting fires in the sanctuary. Father Sabas exhorted his parishioners to prayer and when they asked if he would leave because of fear, he responded, "We must have faith. Aren't we Christians? ... I have been offered the chance to leave and help in other places, but here is where God put me, and here I wait to see what God disposes."

On April 11, he had just completed a Baptism in a private home when federal soldiers arrived and demanded, "Where is the priest?" Serenely, Father Sabas answered, "Here I am."

They tortured him horribly in an attempt to make him tell the hiding place of two other priests. His hands and feet were burned, he was starved, placed in the sun, and given nothing to drink. He was beaten until a number of his bones were broken and his skull was fractured. He suffered the torture with heroic patience. On April 13, 1927 at 9 p.m., he was taken to the cemetery and shot. Three or four times the rifles spoke; each time, Father Reyes rose and cried out "Viva Cristo Rey." One of the soldiers said, "It took much to kill this priest, and he was killed unjustly."

Father Roman Adame

Ordained in 1890, from 1913 until his death Father Adame was the parish priest of Nochistlan, Zacatecas. Here, he founded the Daughters of Mary of Nocturnal Adoration. In his parish ministry, he was especially known for his great charity to the sick. He built chapels in the villages in the surrounding areas. When the persecution began, he continued his ministry in secret. On April 18, 1927, he went to the rancho Veladores to give the Lenten sacraments, where he expressed his sentiments by saying, "What happiness to be a martyr, to give my life for my people."

One of the men of the rancho denounced the priest to Col. Quinones, who arrested Father Adame at dawn of April 19. He was first taken to Mexticacan, and then forced to walk barefoot to Yahualica. One of the soldiers offered his horse when he realized the 68-year-old priest could walk no more. The soldiers of the regiment made fun of this soldier for his compassionate gesture. The Colonel had taken over the priests' residence in Yahualica and during the day Father Adame was kept tied to the columns in front. At night he was thrown in a cell. For three days he was given no food or water. Some countrymen offered to pay a ransom for the priest and the Colonel asked for $6,000. In spite of the fact that they paid the money, on April 21 he was taken to the cemetery to be killed. A grave had already been dug. Antonio Carillo, one of the soldiers from the firing squad, refused to shoot him. The person who testified to seeing the execution could not hear everything clearly. The soldier in charge gave a strong blow in the face to Carillo, and he was shot as well as the priest. The priest raised his hand and pulled back as if to signify that he had completed his duty as the impact of the bullets knocked him directly into the grave.

Father Jose Isabel Flores

Born in Zacatecas in 1866, Father Flores was one of the outstanding alumni of the seminary of Guadalajara. From 1900, he served as the parish priest of Zapotlanejo, Jalisco.

An exemplary priest, he had a great love for the poor, and his ministry was characterized by his kindness and responsibility. He valiantly refused to abandon his parishioners during the worst of the persecution, although he was prudent in exercising his ministry.

The municipal president of town, Jose Orozco, had a great hatred of priests and offered a reward for the capture of any priest in the area. Father Flores was denounced by a man named Nemesio Bermejo, an ex seminarian who lived with him, in order to gain the reward. Father Flores was arrested and offered his freedom if he would accept the Calles laws, but he refused. He was taken to the priest's residence in Zapotlanejo, which had been converted into a jail, where he was held for three days and nights without food or water. Orosco played music outside the prison and told the priest, "You have only to sign Calles's law and I will set you free." The priest responded, "I am going to hear more beautiful music in heaven." When his sister visited him, Father Flores told her, "God knows I am here; this is His Will for me."

On June 21, 1927, he was taken to the municipal cemetery between one and two in the morning, where they began to torture him. He was lassoed around the neck and hung from a tree limb; they lifted him up and down three or four times but the priest didn't say anything. Finally he told his tormentors, "This is not the way you are going to kill me my children; I will tell you how to do it. But before, I want to say that if any of you received from me the sacraments, don't cripple your hands." One of those present said, "I am not going to do this; the priest is my padrino (godfather). He Baptized me." The commander indignantly said, "Well, we will kill you too," to which the man responded, "Then I will die with my padrino." The man was immediately shot. The priest then divided his few possessions among the soldiers. They intended to shoot him, but the guns would not fire, so the commander, Anastasio Valdivia, slit his throat. He was buried immediately in the place where he was killed.

Father Jose Maria Robles

Jose Maria Robles entered the seminary of Guadalajara at the age of 12, and while still a seminarian he began working in Tehuantepec. He was ordained in 1913. Especially devoted to the Heart of Jesus, he founded the congregation of sisters known as the Hermanas del Corazon de Jesus Sacramentado. He was named pastor of Tecolotlan, and during the persecution he exercised his ministry in secret. When many suggested that he leave, he responded, "The shepherd can never abandon his sheep." From January 14, 1927, he celebrated the sacraments in certain houses in secret. During the last five months of his life, he gave admirable proof of his virtues by his study, his prayer, and his Christian mortification. Holy Mass and adoration before the Blessed Sacrament were hallmarks of his life. He tried valiantly to maintain a spiritual Christian life in his parish. June 25, 1927 Colonel Calderon ordered a search of the houses of the town. Father Robles was getting ready to celebrate Mass. He himself opened the door and tranquilly went with the soldiers who took him to the headquarters of the agraristas. Legal defenses were made for his liberty and a stay of execution was obtained. However, at about 10 p.m., he was taken from the jail and murdered close to a nearby rancho. The soldiers took him with his horse near an oak tree, and he knew that his hour had come. He prayed briefly, blessing his parish, pardoning and blessing his murderers. Then he kissed the rope and put it around his neck, and the executioners completed their duty on June 26, 1927.

Father Miguel de la Mora

From 1912 until his death, Father de la Mora served as chaplain of the Cabildo of the Cathedral of Colima. When the persecutions began, he was found and taken prisoner but allowed to leave under bail. When the churches were closed and the public cult suspended in 1926, his friends insisted that he flee with them to the family ranch at El Rincon del Tigre. Father de la

Mora refused, asking them "How can you ask me to leave Colima without a priest?"

General Flores constantly applied psychological pressure to get him to establish a church in opposition to the Catholics, so at last he told his brother he was going to the ranch because he was afraid he would not be able to hold up against the general.

On the way to the ranch, Father and a group of friends stopped at Cardona for breakfast. A woman recognized him as a priest, and asked him to marry her daughter. Some agraristas overheard the conversation, and Father de la Mora and his companions, including his brother, were captured and taken to military headquarters at Colima. General Flores informed the prisoners that he was going to shoot the priest and his brother. On hearing the sentence, Father Miguel took out his rosary and began to recite it. About noon, the soldiers received the order to shoot, and he was killed in front of the horrified eyes of his brother Regino, who was later freed because he had a family to support. Father de la Mora was martyred August 7, 1927 at Cardona, Colima

Father Rodrigo Aguilar

In 1927, Father Aguilar was the acting priest in Union de Tula, Jalisco. At the beginning of the persecution, he said, "The soldiers may take our life, but never our faith."

The priest was full of faith and charity, and a talented poet. From January of 1927, he practiced his ministry in secret. He was hiding at a rancho when he was betrayed and captured by federales under General Izaguirre in October.

At one o'clock in the morning of October 28, 1927 on the orders of the general, he was taken to the main square of Ejutla to be hanged from a mango tree. Taking the rope in his hands, he blessed and forgave his executioners, giving his rosary to one of them. One of the soldiers arrogantly asked, "Who lives?" and told the priest that he wouldn't kill him if he would cry out "Long live the supreme government." Instead, in a firm voice, the priest responded, "Christ the King and Our Lady of Guadalupe." Furiously the rope was pulled to hang him in mid-air. Then he was lowered and again asked, "Who lives?" A second time, without hesitation, the priest responded "Christ the King and our Lady of Guadalupe." A third time he was asked the same question. His answer, with his tongue agonizing in the death throes, remained the same. He was suspended again and died.

Father Margarito Flores

After his ordination in 1924, Father Flores was a professor at the seminary and the vicar of Chilapa, Guerrero. From a poor family, he was always pious and serious, but happy in his ministry. Because of the persecution, he was sent for a time to Mexico City. He was captured in June of 1927, but freed through the influence of the Calvillo family, who obtained his release from General Roberto Cruz. Cruz, it should be noted, was also involved in the execution of Blessed Miguel Pro, S.J. He returned to his diocese at Chilapa.

On hearing of the saintly death of Father Uribe, Father Flores also ardently desired martyrdom, and in October, one day before he returned to Chilapa, he made a holy hour and celebrated a Mass in which he offered his life for the salvation of Mexico.

He put himself at the disposal of the bishop. The bishop could not find a priest willing to go to the parish of Atenango del Rio because the municipal governors had promised to kill any priest who would dare to go there. Father Flores immediately volunteered for the dangerous mission. On November 10, accompanied by a guide, for the sake of prudence, he left to enter the area in a roundabout way. He was identified by government agents, arrested and taken to Tuliman, forced to walk in the blazing sun half naked, barefoot, and tied to the saddle of a horse.

On November 12, 1927, Captain Manzo ordered his execution. Although a ransom was offered, the captain refused to take it. Serenely, Father Flores shared his last meal with the soldiers who held him captive, and about 11 in the morning he was taken to the place of his execution behind the church.

Before the executioners formed up to shoot him, they allowed him to make the sign of the cross over them near the door of the church. As they took him to the place of execution he was praying. When he finished with this, he stepped in front of the soldiers and told them he was ready. They shot him and threw his body in a grave in the cemetery immediately. On exhuming his remains several months later, his blood flowed as if it were fresh. In 1945, his remains were transferred to Taxco.

Father Pedro Esqueda

From his ordination in 1916 until his death, November 22, 1927, Father Pedro Esqueda Ramirez exercised his ministry at San Juan de los Lagos, Jalisco. The center of his life and apostolate was the Holy Eucharist. He organized the association "Cruzada Eucaristica." He especially loved to attend to the catechism and formation of the children making First Communion. During the suspension of public cult, he exercised his ministry in various places without leaving San Juan. To answer the suggestion that he leave, he responded "Dios me trajo, Dios sabra." (God put me here; He knows.) November 17, 1927, in the middle of the night he was in the little room he kept as his oratory where he guarded the Blessed Sacrament and he invited the family of the house to join him in his meditation. He told them, "I am going to make myself ready to die."

On the morning of November 18, Lt. Col. Santoyo and a group of federales surrounded the house. They entered forcibly and found the place under the floorboards where the priest and the sacred vessels were hidden. They took Father Esqueda prisoner, beating him as they left. He was taken to jail and held incommunicado for four days. Each day, he was tortured brutally. Father Esqueda suffered these torments in silence, maintaining a tranquil soul and supporting the torture with resignation.

November 22, 1927, sometimes on foot and sometimes on horseback, but always bound, he was taken to the place of execution where Colonel Santoyo ordered him to climb into a mesquite tree. Father Esqueda attempted to do this several times but was unable because his arm was broken from the torture. Near midday, after more torture, Santoyo shot him.

Father Jesus Mendez

As parish priest of Valtierilla, Michoacan, Father Mendez was devoted to the Eucharist, and he fostered a Eucharistic spirit in his parish. Dedicated to his people, he was assiduous in the confessional, immediate in his attention to the sick, and personally attended the parochial associations.

In 1928 when the federales entered the town, his brother advised him to leave, but he replied, "What happiness to be a martyr. Those of us that die as martyrs are given life in Our Lord."

On February 5, 1928, Father had just given Communion to his sister and another lady at the office of an attorney when they heard shots and fighting outside. He attempted to leave by a back window, taking the chalice under a tilma. He was spotted by a soldier who thought he was carrying arms. On seeing it was only the chalice, they told him they weren't after his jewels, but asked him if he was a priest. He serenely admitted he was. They took him into custody as he hurriedly consumed the hosts. Spying his sister watching, he told her, "Be comforted, this is the Will of God." Turning to the soldiers, he said, "Now you may do to me what you wish; I am ready." The soldiers took him to the town plaza and put him in front of a tree. Three times Captain Munoz attempted to kill him. The first time, he attempted to shoot him, and his pistol malfunctioned. The second time, he ordered the soldiers to fire but no shot hit, possibly because no one wanted to kill him. At last, they removed his medals and cross, and the third volley wounded him. One of the soldiers gave him the coup de grace. The soldiers put his body on the railroad tracks, but the wives of the town officials rescued the body, held a wake, and buried the humble and valiant priest.

Father Toribio Romo

Toribio Romo Gonzalez was born in Jalostotitlan on April 16, 1900 and began attending the seminary at San Juan de Lagos at the age of 13. In 1920, he transferred to the seminary in Guadalajara where he was a good student, a member of Catholic Action, and was distinguished in social work. He was ordained in 1922. He worked in the apostolate with the workmen and propagated eucharistic devotion. For a time, he worked with Father Justino Orona in Cuquio, Jalisco.

Father Romo was assigned to the parish of Tequila, Jalisco in 1927. He set up his living quarters and an oratory in an abandoned factory. Because of the persecution and the ever-present danger, the young priest prayed constantly that God would allow him to have courage and remain without fear. He told his sister, "I am cowardly, but if one day God wants me to be killed, I hope He will give me a rapid death with only the time necessary to pray for my enemies."

On February 23, 1928, he seemed to be very preoccupied and after Mass the next day he told his sister that if anyone came to look for him to tell them he was occupied or a little ill. "I want to put everything in order." He worked all day and night, and when his sister chided him for working too hard, saying he could finish the next day, he insisted on continuing. He finished his work about four in the morning of Sunday the 25th. His eyes were nearly closed with sleep, but the oratory was ready for Mass. He told his sister that he was going to rest a little before celebrating. At 5 a.m. some federale and agrarista troops entered town and forced the mailman to show them where the place of the hidden Mass was. They surprised Father Romo and shot him in his bed. The second volley killed him as he fell into the arms of his sister Maria. The soldiers stripped the priest of his clothing and threw his naked body in front of the city hall in Tequila.

Fathers Justino Orona and Atilano Cruz

Father Orona was the son of an extremely poor family, and after his first studies, he worked for a while in order to help his family. He entered the seminary at Guadalajara in 1894, and he suffered many heartaches while he studied, thinking always of the poverty of his family. He was a good student, held in high esteem by his superiors and his peers, and was ordained in 1904.

As parish priest at Cuquio, he edified everyone by his exemplary conduct, exercising his ministry in spite of anticlericalism and religious indifference in the area. In his parish, he began a religious congregation to care for poor and orphaned young girls. When the persecution increased, he was advised to leave, but he responded, "I am here with my people, live or die." He wrote to a friend, "We must follow the road of our native land with happiness, serving God on earth and giving ourselves for the good of the people. Those of us who walk the road of sorrows with fidelity can leave for Heaven with security."

On June 28, 1928, he went to the Rancho Las Cruces, the home of the Jimenez-Loza family, along with his brother Josemaria and Torribio Ayala. Ayala was a self-effacing Christian. For his "crime" of assisting the priest, he himself was hung shortly after the assassination of the priest. The following day, Father Orona's vicar, Father Atiliano Cruz, joined them. They wanted to plan how to carry on their ministry during the dangers of the persecution.

Father Atilano Cruz Alvarado was a young priest, only 26 years old, who had just been ordained in 1927. On his arrival at the rancho, he and the pastor recited the rosary together and then stayed up late, making plans for their pastoral ministry. When Father Orona asked Father Cruz if he were not afraid of the government, Father Cruz replied that he would greet them with the words, "Long Live Christ the King."

At dawn on the first of July, some federales under Captain Vega along with the municipal president of Cuquio broke into the house where the two priests were sleeping. Father Cruz opened the door of his room and greeted them with the words "Viva Cristo Rey" in a strong clear voice. Father Orona was killed immediately; Father Cruz was mortally wounded. The bodies of both were thrown on the patio of the house and afterward were taken to the main plaza of town and left there. The faithful took the bodies and buried them in the cemetery of Cuquio.

Father Tranquilino Ubiarco

Under Carranza, the seminaries were closed, so Tranquilino continued his education in private homes. He was ordained in 1923, and sent to the parish of Tepatitlan. A zealous pastor, he established a Christian newspaper to teach the faithful and began a soup kitchen for the poor and the refugees from the persecution. This area was a common place for battles between the Cristeros and the government forces, so his ministry was carried out in hiding.

In March of 1928, he told a group of young girls that he had asked for the grace of giving his life for Christ. The night of October 4, he spent in a private home where early in the morning he was going to celebrate Mass and perform a wedding. The next morning after Mass, he was arrested and thrown in a cell with some other men. He heard their confessions and led them in saying the rosary. Two hours later, Colonel Lacarra ordered that he parade around the sidewalk and enter town. Before he left, he asked the soldiers which one was commissioned to kill him. When all remained silent, he said, "All of this is God's will; the man who is made to kill me is not responsible." One of the soldiers then said he was the one chosen, but he couldn't do it. Later, Father asked with what instrument he would be killed. They told him he would be hanged, and with total tranquility he blessed them. They hung him from a branch of a eucalyptus tree at the entrance of town. The soldier in charge of the execution refused to carry out the order, so he, himself, was shot on the same day.

Pedro de Jesus Maldonado

Pedro de Jesus Maldonado Lucero entered the seminary of Chihuahua at the age of seventeen, but in 1914, because of the political conflict, classes were suspended and he dedicated himself to learning music. Eventually, he was able to finish his studies and was ordained in El Paso, Texas in 1918. In 1924, he was named pastor of Santa Isabel, Chihuahua. In his priestly ministry, he was especially dedicated to the catechism of the children, he increased night adoration, and he established many Marian associations in his parish.

During the intense persecution in the years from 1926 to 1929, he continued his ministry in his parish, cementing the faith of his parishioners and inculcating in them a love and respect for the Holy Father and his legitimate priests.

In 1931, the persecution recurred in Chihuahua and the churches were again closed. Father Maldonado was detained in 1932 and released, and in 1934 he was arrested again. He was imprisoned, mistreated, threatened and sent back across the border to El Paso. Here he stayed in safety for some time, but his heart was with his parish and he begged his bishop to be allowed to return as his sheep were without their shepherd. At last the bishop gave his permission and Father Maldonado returned to exercise his ministry in the townships and villages of his parish. There was a fire in the public school, and the authorities blamed the priest. On February 10, 1937, a group of armed and drunken men arrested him at his house and made him walk barefoot to Santa Isabel. He recited his rosary along the way. He was taken to the city hall where the municipal chiefs beat him up, hitting him on the head with the butt of a rifle so hard that it dislocated his left eye and knocked him out.

At a holy hour shortly before his death, he had prayed for the grace of receiving final communion before his death. He had the sacred host with him in a reliquary, and when his murderers found it, Jesus Salcido forced him to eat it saying, "Eat this, this is your last communion!" They beat him again and again with their rifle butts until he was unconscious, bathed in his innocent blood. They then took him to the Civil Hospital of Chihuahua where he died on February 11, 1937.

Ann Ball is a businesswoman and Catholic writer whose specialty is the modern saints and Catholic tradition and heritage. She is also a frequent contributor to The Word Among Us and various Our Sunday Visitor publications. Ann lives in Houston, Texas.

Courage and Youth:
Blessed Pedro Calungsod

By Kathryn Lively

"At a young age, Blessed Pedro heard the call of Christ and never wavered in his desire to do God's will, even at the cost of his life," Pope John Paul II told a crowd of more than 30,000 assembled at the Vatican for beatification ceremonies on March 5, 2000. "Let us pray that many young people will follow Blessed Pedro's example and give themselves to the Lord in the many forms of lay apostolate or in the priesthood and religious life."

The martyr of whom the Pontiff spoke was Blessed Pedro Calungsod, one of 44 martyrs of various heritages and eras beatified that day, the first such martyr raised to the altars of the Church to have come from Visaya in the Archdiocese of Cebu, a small island in the Philippines. Despite the dearth of personal information on Calungsod, whose martyrdom in the 17th century marked a dark period in the Church's history in the East Indies, certain religious were not deterred from pursuing Calungsod's cause, nor did it prevent over five thousand Filipinos from gathering in St. Peter's Square to celebrate the occasion, all dressed in blue and waving the country's flag.

What is known about the brief life of Calungsod is told traditionally through tales of another fellow martyr, Spaniard Diego Luis de San Vitores. When he was but fourteen, Calungsod volunteered to accompany San Vitores, a Jesuit priest, and others to the Marianas Islands to help evangelize the Christian faith to the natives. His heart full of love for Christ and enthusiastic about sharing the Gospel, Calungsod boarded the *San Diego* and landed with the crew and missionaries just off the shores of Agana in Guam in 1668.

Guam, claimed for the Spanish as a port of call in the 1500s following an expedition by Miguel Lopez de Legazpi, was populated primarily by the Chamorro tribe. Unlike the male-dominated European society, the Chamarros were dominated by women, and the *maga'hagas*, were involved in all of the tribe's important decisions and were the only people on the island permitted to inherit land. The highest-ranking male of this tribe, the *maga'lahi*, was Chief Kepuha, seen by the foreign missionaries as a hardy, muscular man who did have some authority in tribal matters, so long as the *maga'hagas* consented to his decisions.

It is a certainty that the *maga'hagas* approved of conversion to Christianity among the Chamarros upon the arrival of the missionaries, as Kepuha embraced the new faith and was baptized by San Vitores. By the following year, Calungsod and the Jesuits established *Dulce Nombre de Maria*, or Sweet Name of Mary Cathedral Basilica, Guam's first Catholic Church, built on land offered by Kepuha, following permission from the *maga'hagas*. Although Kepuha would die the following year, relations between the missionaries and the Chamarros were civil, with San Vitores and Calungsod preaching the Gospel to anyone willing to listen.

Two years later, however, the presence of the Spanish and Filipino foreigners was quickly seen as an unwanted intrusion by certain tribal members. Chief Hurao likened the missionaries' Christian evangelization to an attempt to eradicate their culture. "They dare to take away our liberty, which should be dearer to us than life itself," Hurao declared in a stirring speech meant to incite his people to revolution. "They try to persuade us that we will be happier, and some of us had been blinded into believing their words."

Hurao's dissatisfaction with the foreigners extended beyond matters of faith. San Vitores and his followers, Hurao believed, had brought more than just the Word of God to Guam. They brought new diseases which the Chamarros could not remedy, prejudices which would make a normal native islander suddenly shameful of his naked appearance, and an air of superiority that nettled under the chief's skin. The Chamarros were fine before the missionaries arrived, Hurao reasoned to his people, and they could be happy again with them gone.

On April 2, 1672, Hurao used what appeared to be an innocent turn of events as a catalyst for freeing his people from outside influence. San Vitores had baptized the infant daughter of Chief Mata'pang. Mata'pang opposed the baptism, though as a male he had no say in the matter, and it is believed today that the child's mother consented. Nevertheless, Mata'pang, angered with the prospect of having to be loyal to a Spanish monarch and convinced that the holy water used in the Christian baptisms was poisoning Chamarro children, agreed to take measures against the missionaries. San Vitores and Calungsod were murdered, both stabbed with a bone-tip lance.

Despite Hurao's belief that the natives could overpower the Spanish based upon the advantage of tribal numbers as opposed to quality of weaponry, the relatively peaceful Chamarros quickly became the target of a vengeful feud that ravaged the island for the next twenty-five years. The peaceful ministry of San Vitores, Calungsod and the Jesuits was soon forgotten as the Spanish military mercilessly raged against the natives, killing as many as 200,000 people between 1670 and 1695, including Mata'pang. When the dust settled, the remaining Chamarros found themselves being integrated involuntarily into Spanish culture, forced into attending daily Mass, speaking Spanish and dressing in European fashion.

Though it would appear that this period in Guam's history would forever tarnish the image of the Church, the faith and courage of those first Jesuit missionaries were never forgotten. Nearly three centuries after his execution, San Vitores was beatified on October 6, 1985 as a martyr for the Faith. As San Vitores's story became more widely known in the areas where the slain Jesuit priest ministered, a desire to see the merits of his companions recognized by the Church grew. In Cebu, that tiny birthplace of San Vitores's young assistant who willingly hopped aboard a ship without so much as thought of himself, Archbishop Ricardo Cardinal Vidal helped open the cause for Calungsod's beatification.

A decade's worth of hard work paid off for the small Visayan community who may now declare one of their own in Heaven. "Pedro Calungsod's star will now shine brightly in our Philippine skies," declared Jamie Cardinal Sin. "Pedro Calungsod's death speaks of conviction, commitment, the gift of self, unto the end."

Kathryn Lively is a graduate of Jacksonville University and a freelance writer whose work has appeared in various trade and literary magazines. A native of Jacksonville, Florida, she currently lives in Virginia.

Tim Drake

Canonizations

Tim Drake

Witnesses at Fatima:

Jacinta and Francisco Marto

By Kathryn Mulderink

"Unless you change and become like little children you will never enter the Kingdom of Heaven" (Mt. 18:3). The words of Christ Himself exalt the active role that little ones can have in the Kingdom of God. The May 13, 2000 beatifications of these two young seers from the tiny village of Fatima, Portugal – the youngest non-martyrs to be declared blessed by the Church – speak to us of the simplicity and totality of their "yes" to the Virgin Mother; a simplicity and totality that serves as an example to all.

Although a private revelation, Fatima contains a message for all of mankind, particularly in the last century of the second millennium, so marked by war, violence, persecution, despair and attacks against the life of the unborn and the family. "...(Fatima) prophesized the tribulations of these times and the Virgin asked for prayers to shorten these evils."[1] In the eight decades since the apparitions took place, millions have recognized its universality and relevance. "From Fatima, the message of conversion and hope spread all over the world. It is a message that, in conformity with Christian revelation, is deeply inserted into history. Coming from lived experiences, it invites believers to pray fervently for peace in the world and to do penance so that hearts will be open to conversion. This is the genuine Gospel of Christ re-proposed to our generation, particularly tested by past events. The appeal that God makes to us by means of the Blessed Virgin is still current today."[2]

Prior to the events of the spring and summer of 1917, there was nothing to draw the attention of the world to the poor mountain hamlet of Fatima, in the middle of Portugal. Nor was there much to distinguish Jacinta and Francisco, the two youngest children of Manuel Pedro Marto and Olimpia de Jesus dos Santos, from the other village children. At ages 7 and 9 they displayed a certain degree of ethical seriousness that was ordinary for children brought up in a family and village with deep Christian roots. Honesty was a fundamental norm in the upbringing of the family, a norm which was to cause so much suffering to the children, when insinuations were later made that the story of the apparitions was a lie made up by them.

---

[1] John Paul II, Beatification homily, May 13, 2000
[2] John Paul II, May 13, 2000

Jacinta was a lively and joyful child, with a love for singing and dancing. She was well-liked by the other children, despite her tendency to be possessive and a bit moody. In fact, their cousin and constant companion, Lucia admitted, "I sometimes found Jacinta's company quite disagreeable, on account of her over-sensitive temperament. The slightest quarrel which arose among the children when at play was enough to send her pouting into a corner..."[3]

Her brother Francisco was more docile and serious than she, with a sensitive and sympathetic temperament. He was so unlike his younger sister that, "apart from his features and his practice of virtue, Francisco did not seem at all to be Jacinta's brother. Unlike her, he was neither capricious nor vivacious. On the contrary, he was quiet and submissive by nature...I must confess that I myself did not always feel too kindly disposed towards him, as his naturally calm temperament exasperated my own excessive vivacity."[4]

The three cousins spent much of their time watching their parents' sheep. While the flocks grazed, the little shepherds played games, sang songs, and said their rosary. But prayers were not as popular as play, so the cousins, impatient to get back to their games, devised a way to get the rosary said much faster. Instead of reciting the complete prayers, they would simply run their fingers across the beads saying the first two words of each prayer: "Our Father, Hail Mary, Hail Mary, Hail Mary."

Then, in 1916, an angel appeared to them three times. He taught them several prayers and exhorted them to pray continually. He also asked them to offer sacrifices in reparation for the sins by which God is offended, and to obtain the conversion of sinners. "The words of the angel were like a light which made us understand who and what God really is – how He loves us and wishes to be loved," wrote Lucia. [5] Their transformation in Christ begun, the children began to offer everything to God and to spend long hours praying as the Angel had taught them, with their foreheads touching the ground, in the manner of many Orthodox Christians. More and more, they wanted only to love and please God.

Far from Fatima, events which would effect the world were taking place. Just a few years earlier, in 1914, Russia had finally succeeded in assassinating Grigorii Rasputin, the mysterious monk who had controlled the Czarina and scandalized the country for a decade. The imperialist government was soon to collapse in the face of starvation, poverty, and demonstrations. In March of 1917, the first Russian revolution took place, overthrowing the thousand-year-old monarchy and replacing it with a

---

[3] Fr. Louis Kondor, ed., *Fatima in Lucia's Own Words*, (Fatima Portugal, 1976), p. 20.

[4] Kondor, p. 124.

[5] Fr. John de Marchi,, *True Story of Fatima*, (St. Paul, 1952), p. 43.

moderate, democratically oriented regime. Russians were optimistic, and most world observers expected the revolution to help the country emerge from its backwardness. In April, Lenin (who was exiled in Switzerland) was transported back to Russia through the heart of wartime Germany in the famous "sealed train" – a railroad car which the Germans carefully isolated from all contacts with the populace, to prevent the spread of any dangerous doctrines within their own borders. As leader of the Bolsheviks he would soon spread his Marxist message throughout Russia and the world, even though the Bolsheviks were one of the smallest parties, numbering no more than twenty thousand out of a population of one hundred million. No one could have foreseen the disastrous consequences Lenin's meteoric rise to power would have for the world. By November, the Bolsheviks would stage their own revolution and usher in a dark era in modern history. And during the six months between revolutions, a Mother was preparing her children.

The First World War was approaching the end of its third year in May of 1917, and every diplomatic gesture toward peace had failed. It was on the fifth of that month, the month of Mary, that Pope Benedict XV issued an appeal for a world crusade of prayer to the Heart of Jesus through Our Lady for an early peace. Only eight days later, on May 13 (the feast of Our Lady of the Blessed Sacrament, as declared by Pope Pius X in 1905), as Jacinta, Francisco, and Lucia tended their flocks in the Cova da Iria, a beautiful Lady appeared to them, shining with light. She told them that she was from Heaven, and that she would come on the 13th day of the next five months. After promising them that they would go to Heaven, she put to them an extraordinary question: *"Do you wish to offer up to God all the sufferings He desires to send you, in reparation for the sins by which He is offended, and in supplication for the conversion of sinners?"*

And in an equally extraordinary answer we observe the result of a mystical experience that transformed their souls and filled them with wisdom beyond their years: "Yes, we do."

"Go then. You will have much to suffer, but God's grace will comfort you."

Here we have the fundamental elements of the spirituality of the seers. The other apparitions developed and characterized these elements, but the essential message was revealed in this first dialogue. The response is given spontaneously, with charming simplicity and profound generosity: "Yes, we do." "It is the 'yes' of the creature to the proposal of God, the 'yes' of freedom and surrender that marks the course of an entire life… It is a total surrender of the creature into the hands of the Creator."[6]

---

[6] D. Francisco Rendeiro, Bishop of Coimbra, Homily given at Fatima, March 13, 1970

The sufferings foretold by the Blessed Virgin began immediately, when Jacinta was unable to keep the secret and told of the beautiful Lady to her mother. Both her parents and Lucia's accused the children of making up fanciful lies, despite their insistence that they were telling the truth, and very soon the neighbors were mocking them as well; it was indeed a heavy cross to bear.

After the first apparition, these two young shepherds were profoundly changed. The very next day, as Lucia relates, this transformation was apparent. "When we reached the pasture, Jacinta sat thoughtfully on a rock, refusing to play. 'Because I'm thinking. That Lady told us to say the Rosary and to make sacrifices for the conversion of sinners. So from now on, when we say the Rosary we must say the whole Hail Mary and the whole Our Father! And the sacrifices, how are we going to make them?' Right away, Francisco thought of a good sacrifice: 'Let's give our lunch to the sheep, and make the sacrifice of doing without it.'"[7]

They devised many ways to make the reparation requested by the Lady, including refusing to drink water, even during the heat of the summer. On one occasion, Lucia encouraged them to take a drink.

Francisco answered, "I don't want to...I want to suffer for the conversion of sinners."

"The heat was getting more and more intense. The shrill singing of the crickets and grasshoppers coupled with the croaking of the frogs in the neighboring pond made an uproar that was almost unbearable. Jacinta, frail as she was, and weakened still more by the lack of food and drink, said to me with that simplicity which was natural to her: 'Tell the crickets and the frogs to keep quiet! I have such a terrible headache.'

Then Francisco asked her: 'Don't you want to suffer this for sinners?'

The poor child, clasping her head between her two little hands, replied: 'Yes I do. Let them sing!'"[8]

The rest of their short lives were focused on making reparation for sinners and consoling Our Lord. Lucia testifies to this: "Jacinta took this matter of making sacrifices for the conversion of sinners so much to heart, that she never let a single opportunity escape her... (Her) thirst for making sacrifices seemed insatiable."[9]

Their means of sacrifice ranged from eating bitter acorns and olives for lunch, to wearing a rope around their waists, and finally, suffering courageously the martyrdom of misunderstanding, illness, and death. Their encounter with the Blessed Virgin instilled in them a burning love for God,

---

[7] Kondor, p. 29
[8] Kondor, p. 34
[9] Kondor, p. 30, 31

from which was born the sacrificial love for souls that attained heroic heights.

After two priests who came to question them recommended that they pray for the Holy Father, the children grew to love him deeply. Jacinta's devotion was so great that it seems she was rewarded with special favors. One day, as the children were resting, Jacinta called out, "Didn't you see the Holy Father?" When they said they had not, she explained that she saw him kneeling by a table, with his head in his hands, weeping. Outside the house there were many people cursing and throwing stones.

Another time, Jacinta saw many roads full of people crying with hunger, and the Pope in a church praying before the Immaculate Heart of Mary with many other people. These visions inspired her to pray with greater intensity for the Holy Father.

On June 13, the Portuguese observe the feast day of St. Anthony with great celebrations. But even this was not enough to keep the children from returning to the Cova on the day appointed by the Lady for her second appearance. During the apparition, Lucia asked, "What do you want of me?" Our Lady told her she wanted her to learn to read and write. She also told the children that Jacinta and Francisco would be taken to heaven soon, but that Lucia would need to remain *"a little longer, since Jesus wishes you to make me known and loved on earth. He wishes also for you to establish devotion in the world to my Immaculate Heart."* Our Lady opened her hands and communicated to the children a great light in which they could see themselves, as if submerged in God Himself. Witnesses to this apparition saw, few inches from the tree, a cloud which rose very slowly and moved toward the east until it was no longer visible.

In July, as the Allies were launching the Passchendaele Offensive, the climax of the horror of the military side of WWI, the Lady came again and gave them a three-part secret. The first two parts were revealed in 1941, in memoirs Lucia had written under obedience to the Bishop of Leiria:

> Our Lady showed us a great sea of fire which seemed to be under the earth. Plunged in this fire were demons and souls in human form, like transparent burning embers, all blackened or burnished bronze, floating about in the conflagration, now raised into the air by the flames that issued from within themselves together with great clouds of smoke, now falling back on every side like sparks in a huge fire, without weight or equilibrium, and amid shrieks and groans of pain and despair, which horrified us and made us tremble with fear. The demons could be distinguished by their terrifying and repulsive likeness to frightful and

unknown animals, all black and transparent. This vision lasted but an instant. How can we ever be grateful enough to our kind heavenly Mother, who had already prepared us by promising, in the first Apparition, to take us to heaven. Otherwise, I think we would have died of fear and terror.

We then looked up at Our Lady, who said to us so kindly and so sadly:

You have seen hell where the souls of poor sinners go. To save them, God wishes to establish in the world devotion to my Immaculate Heart. If what I say to you is done, many souls will be saved and there will be peace. The war is going to end: but if people do not cease offending God, a worse one will break out during the Pontificate of Pius XI. When you see a night illumined by an unknown light, know that this is the great sign given you by God that he is about to punish the world for its crimes, by means of war, famine, and persecutions of the Church and of the Holy Father. To prevent this, I shall come to ask for the consecration of Russia to my Immaculate Heart, and the Communion of reparation on the First Saturdays. If my requests are heeded, Russia will be converted, and there will be peace; if not, she will spread her errors throughout the world, causing wars and persecutions of the Church. The good will be martyred; the Holy Father will have much to suffer; various nations will be annihilated. In the end, my Immaculate Heart will triumph. The Holy Father will consecrate Russia to me, and she shall be converted, and a period of peace will be granted to the world.

The third part remained a secret to the world until the beatification ceremonies on May 13, 2000. It was there that a disclosure was made as to the nature of this "secret" and the full text, written in Lucia's hand, was released within a few weeks:

After the two parts which I have already explained, at the left of Our Lady and a little above, we saw an Angel with a flaming sword in his left hand; flashing, it gave out flames that looked as though they would set the world on fire; but they died out in contact with the splendor that Our Lady radiated towards him from her right hand: pointing to the earth with his right hand, the Angel cried out in a loud

40

voice: '<u>Penance</u>, <u>Penance</u>, <u>Penance</u>!'. And we saw in an immense light that is God: 'something similar to how people appear in a mirror when they pass in front of it' a Bishop dressed in White 'we had the impression that it was the Holy Father'. Other Bishops, Priests, men and women Religious going up a steep mountain, at the top of which there was a big Cross of rough-hewn trunks as of a cork-tree with the bark; before reaching there the Holy Father passed through a big city half in ruins and half trembling with halting step, afflicted with pain and sorrow, he prayed for the souls of the corpses he met on his way; having reached the top of the mountain, on his knees at the foot of the big Cross he was killed by a group of soldiers who fired bullets and arrows at him, and in the same way there died one after another the other Bishops, Priests, men and women Religious, and various lay people of different ranks and positions. Beneath the two arms of the Cross there were two Angels each with a crystal aspersorium in his hand, in which they gathered up the blood of the Martyrs and with it sprinkled the souls that were making their way to God. Tuy-3-1-1944.

During this vision, a stream of light came from the Lady's opened hands and penetrated into the hearts of the children.

"What made the most powerful impression on (Francisco) and what wholly absorbed him, was God, the Most Holy Trinity, perceived in that light which penetrated our inmost souls. Afterwards, he said: ' We were on fire in that light which is God, and yet we were not burnt! What is God? We could never put it into words. Yes, that is something indeed, which we could never express! But what a pity it is that He is so sad! If only I could console Him!'"[10]

"From that day onwards, our hearts were filled with a more ardent love for the Immaculate Heart of Mary. From time to time, Jacinta said to me: 'The Lady said that her Immaculate Heart will be your refuge and the way that will lead you to God. Don't you love that? Her Heart is so good! How I love it!'"[11]

By now, thousands of people throughout the country of Portugal had heard about the happenings at Fatima and crowds were coming to the Cova to pray. Many of them wanted to speak with the children, ask them

---

[10]Kondor, p. 132-3

[11] Kondor, p. 112

questions, or give them petitions to present to the Lady. This too was a great cross for the children, who often hid from the many visitors. The government, which in 1910 had a change of leadership and was now determined to obliterate religion, did not look kindly on stories of miracles. On the 13th of August, as they were heading out toward the Cova, the Mayor lured the children away under the ruse of offering them a ride. He took them to his home and locked them in a room, telling them they would not be freed until they confided their precious secret. But the children would not tell him. The following day the mayor tried bribing, charming, threatening. Still nothing. In the afternoon they were put in the public jail with adult criminals. Intent on getting the children to change their story about seeing the Lady, the Mayor threatened to boil the children in oil, one at a time. Feeling alone and abandoned, they remained strong, facing their certain death courageously, as it would only bring them to Heaven sooner. They offered their sufferings to God and persuaded the prisoners to join them in prayer. When the mayor's threats failed to extract the secret from the little shepherds, they were released.

A few days later, on the 19th of August, when the children were tending their flocks at Valinhos, the Lady appeared to the children and told them to return to the Cova on the 13th of September, promising that "on the 13th of October I will work a great miracle so that everyone will believe." After the brief vision ended, there was a noticeable perfume in the air. The children snapped off fragrant branches from the holm oak and took them home to their families, explaining that these were the branches touched by Our Lady's feet. The fragrance, though unidentifiable, was beautiful.

Again in September, thousands gathered to ask the children to intercede for them to the Lady. As noon approached, many saw a luminous globe coming from the sky, and a white cloud surrounding the children. Many of the onlookers also saw a shower of small white petals fall from the sky, which vanished when they reached the ground.

News of the coming miracle spread far and wide, and thousands of people began coming to the Cova, many days before the 13th of October. For most, it was a long and arduous journey, and the same terrible storm endured by the soldiers fighting and dying in Flanders during the "Campaign in the Mud" raged for days over the little hamlet. The Cova and the land around Fatima were a mass of mud and puddles. Lucia's mother, fearing there would be no miracle at all and the crowds would kill her daughter, insisted that Lucia go to confession.

When the children reached the Cova that morning, more than 70,000 believers and skeptics had gathered, making it almost impossible to reach the little holm oak. After making their way slowly through the crowds, the children knelt in prayer, and the Lady appeared at the Cova for the last time.

At last, they would learn from her own lips who she was. "I am the Lady of the Rosary. I would like a chapel built here in my honor. Continue to pray the Rosary every day."

Then she opened her arms and a great ray of light extended from them into the sun. Lucia cried out, "Look at the sun!" As the people looked up, the dark clouds disappeared and the sun began to spin like a giant wheel, casting off beautiful rays of light, like a spinning rainbow. Then it seemed to hurl itself toward the ground. The people fell to their knees, some fearing the end of the world had come, others in awe and prayer. There was no place to run.

But just before it seemed it would strike the earth, the blazing sun abruptly came to a halt and hovered over the heads of the crowd. Then it very slowly returned to its place in the heavens. As the crowd was watching the frightful spectacle, the children saw in the sun the Holy Family with St. Joseph and the Child Jesus making the Sign of the Cross over the whole world; then Our Lady of Sorrows with Our Lord again blessing the world; and finally, Our Lady of Mt. Carmel, witnessed by Lucia alone. When the crowd finally stopped staring at the sky, they realized that their clothes and the ground, which were soaked only minutes before by days of rainfall, were now completely dry. With one voice they shouted, "A miracle! A miracle!" The crowd's enthusiasm was then directed at the children; Jacinta had to be carried away to safety while Lucia's veil and dress were torn and her hair was cut for souvenirs. The newspaper *O Seculo* described the 12-minute event, saying, "The sun has danced."

Within a year of the final apparition, the Spanish flu raged throughout the land, taking many lives. Francisco and Jacinta were both taken ill, and while their sufferings were intense, they bore them patiently in reparation and for the love of Jesus and Mary. Our Lady visited them and told them that she would soon take Francisco to heaven, but that Jacinta would first suffer in two hospitals before dying alone. During her illness, Jacinta continued her contemplative prayer. Lucia's aunt made this request: " 'Ask Jacinta what she is thinking, when she covers her face with her hands and remains motionless for such a long while. I've already asked her, but she just smiles and does not answer.'" Lucia put the question to Jacinta, who replied: "'I think of Our Lord, of Our Lady, of sinners, and of...(and she mentioned certain parts of the Secret). I love to think.'" [12]

On April 4, 1919, Francisco became the first of the three seers to reach heaven. Shortly thereafter Jacinta's condition worsened and she was hospitalized in a local hospital. Later, she was moved to another hospital in Lisbon. While there, she said, "If men knew what eternity means, they

---

[12] Kondor, p. 44

would change their way of life." About a month before her death, while doctors tried in vain to save Jacinta's life, she clasped the Reverend Mother's hand and said, "I have seen Our Lady again. She has taken all the pain away." On Friday, February 20, 1920, Our Lady kept her promise to come and take Jacinta to Heaven. There was a delay of several days in arranging for Jacinta's burial, allowing many people to come and see her body, and many testified to the pinkness of her cheeks and the beautiful fragrance her body exhaled.

"We can certainly include the Servants of God, Francisco and Jacinta Marto, among the children who responded most readily to Jesus' love and affection for them. The gifts of grace which were granted to them bore fruit abundantly in them, so much so that in a few years they attained a great perfection in the following of Christ and in the practice of the Christian virtues. In spite of their tender age, they have left us a splendid example of obedience to the will of God, of burning love for the Immaculate Heart of Mary, and of a deep desire to console Our Lord, so offended by the sins of men, and to pray and suffer for the needs of the Church and for the conversion of sinners."[13] In the words of the Holy Father: "It was the heroism of children, but it was true heroism."[14]

The story of Fatima certainly does not end with the death of the two youngest seers. While the visions took place during a pivotal moment in history, history moves forward and events continue to unfold which point back to those months in 1917, when the events were only local news. Lucia continued to be blessed with visions from Heaven, directing her and shedding light on other events.

On June 13, 1929, she was shown the famous vision of the Blessed Trinity, and was told the time had come for the collegial Consecration to the Immaculate Heart of Mary. This consecration took several forms and only gradually was the total consecration made. Pius XII (whose episcopal ordination took place on May 13, 1917 and who was buried on October 13, 1958) made the consecration in 1942 without mentioning Russia specifically and again in 1952 with specific mention of Russia, but not collegially. On May 13, 1946, he had Our Lady of Fatima crowned Queen of the Word by a papal legate. There were no further attempts to make the consecration as requested until 1967, when Paul VI renewed the consecration of Pius XII, and sent a golden rose to Fatima, in recognition of the apparitions. But while this consecration was made in the presence of the bishops, it was not made in union with them. Again, attempts to fulfill the requirements of the

---

[13] Decree of May 13, 1989 concerning the Heroicity of the Virtues of the Servants of God

[14] John Paul II, statements in Rome, May 17, 2000

consecration seemed to be on hold and some began to believe that the relevance of Fatima had waned after World War II.

Then Pope John Paul II was elected Pope, choosing for his motto "Totus Tuus" and bringing the Blessed Mother again to the forefront. On May 13, 1981, an attempt was made on his life while he was greeting the crowds in St. Peter's square. At the moment he was shot, the Holy Father had bent forward to look more closely at an image of Our Lady of Fatima, which someone in the crowd was holding up to him. Because of this, the bullet missed his central aorta by a few millimeters, and his life was spared. It was no coincidence, the Pope later affirmed, that the shooting occurred on the feast of Our Lady of Fatima. When the Pope went to visit his would-be killer in prison, Ali Acga asked the Pope why he didn't die. The Holy Father answered, "One hand fired the shot. Another guided it."

In his own words, "I had already intended for some time to come to Fatima...But after the attempt on my life, on regaining consciousness, my thought turned immediately to (Fatima), to place in the heart of the heavenly Mother my thanks for having saved me from danger. I saw in everything that was happening...a special motherly protection of Our Lady. And... I also saw an appeal and a reminder of the message which came...65 years ago." While recuperating in Gemelli Hospital in Rome, the Holy Father read both the secret of Fatima and the diary of Sr. Faustina Kowalska. He immediately made plans to make the consecration and entrust the world to the mercy of God through His Mother.

On May 13, 1982, John Paul II went to Fatima and again consecrated the world to the Immaculate Heart of Mary, but although he had sent letters to all the bishops so that they could make the consecration with him, not all had received their letters on time. Lucia herself said that this did not fulfill all of the requirements of Our Blessed Mother. Finally, in 1984, John Paul II sent letters to all the bishops, including Orthodox bishops and leading Protestants, and invited them to make the consecration in union with him on March 25.[15] The statue from the Fatima shrine was brought to St. Peter's square and an all-night vigil was held the night before. Lucia confirmed that this collegial consecration was indeed accepted by Our Lord.[16]

The timeline of grace is stunning. In March, 1985, Mikhail Gorbachev became President of Russia and introduced "perestroika" and "glasnost", policies which encouraged greater freedom and openness, allowing religion to be practiced again, and leading eventually to the downfall of Communism in that country.

---

[15] Fr. Robert Fox, EWTN
[16] Archbishop Tarcisio Bertone, Secy of the Congregation for the Doctrine of the Faith, statement released with the "Third Secret"

On May 13, 1989, the two young seers were declared Venerable. The following year, Mikhail Gorbachev visited John Paul II in Rome, and both later said that they were friends from that first meeting.

On May 13, 1991, John Paul II returned to Fatima to thank Our Lady again for sparing his life and for the many countries that were rejecting Communism, saying "we are at the dawn of a new springtime of Christianity." Three months later, on yet another anniversary of a Fatima apparition, August 19, 1991, the hard-line Communists, seeing what Gorbachev had wrought, tried to get rid of him by staging a coup. But by August 22 (Feast of the Queenship of Mary), the coup was over and Gorbachev was back in control; on December 25, the red flag over the Kremlin came down for the last time. Soon, Gorbachev resigned as President and, the same day, sent a letter to his friend, John Paul II. Finally, one year later, on Christmas 1992, Communism officially ended in Russia.

Does this mean the message of Fatima has finally lost its relevance?

"The vision of Fatima concerns above all the war waged by atheist systems against the Church and Christians, and it describes the immense suffering endured by the witnesses to the faith in the last century of the second millennium. It is an interminable Way of the Cross led by the Popes of the twentieth century...Even if the events to which the third part of the secret of Fatima refers now seem part of the past, Our Lady's call to conversion and penance, issued at the beginning of the twentieth century, remains timely and urgent today."[17]

It seems clear, in light of the revelation of the third secret, that John Paul II is the Pope foreseen by Jacinta. John Paul II himself said at the beatification ceremony: ""I wished to celebrate once more the goodness of the Lord to me; when gravely wounded on that May 13, 1981, he saved my life. I also express my appreciation to Blessed Jacinta for the sacrifices and prayers offered for the Holy Father, whom she saw suffer so much." When the Bishop of Leiria-Fatima visited Rome, the Pope gave him the very bullet used in the assassination attempt, so that it might be kept at the shrine – a powerful statement by a man who "halted at the threshold of death." The Bishop decided it should be set, like a precious stone, in the crown of the statue of Our Lady of Fatima.

Another powerful statement came on October 7-8, 2000, when Pope John Paul II entrusted the Third Millennium to Our Lady of Fatima.[18] The statue of Our Lady of Fatima from the Chapel of the Apparitions at the Fatima sanctuary in Portugal was brought to St. Peter's Basilica in Rome for the special event. On the Feast of Our Lady of the Rosary, a large crowd

---

[17] Cardinal Sodano, statements made at beatification ceremony, May 13, 2000

[18] Archbishop Crescenzio Sepe, Secy. Gen. of the Vatican Jubilee Committee, statement of March 22, 2000

gathered to join the Holy Father in praying the Rosary before the statue. Bishops from around the world, in Rome for the Jubilee Year participated in the entrustment at the end of an October 8 Mass in St. Peter's Basilica.

The text of that entrustment echoed the Acts of Entrustment made by John Paul II in 1981, 1982, and 1984, which contained these heartfelt words:

> Behold, as we stand before...your Immaculate Heart, we desire, together with the whole Church, to unite ourselves with the consecration which, for love of us, your Son made of himself to the Father: 'For their sake,' he said, 'I consecrate myself that they also may be consecrated in truth' (Jn 17:19). We wish to unite ourselves with our Redeemer in this his consecration for the world and for the human race, which, in his divine Heart, has the power to obtain pardon and to secure reparation.
>
> The power of this consecration lasts for all time and embraces all individuals, peoples and nations. It overcomes every evil that the spirit of darkness is able to awaken, and has in fact awakened in our times, in the heart of man and in his history....
>
> Let there be revealed, once more, in the history of the world the infinite saving power of the Redemption: the power of Merciful Love! May it put a stop to evil! May it transform consciences! May your Immaculate Heart reveal for all the light of Hope![19]

---

[19] Archbishop Tarcisio Bertone, Secy of the Congregation for the Doctrine of the Faith, statement released with the "Third Secret"

Tim Drake

Maria Josefa
of the Heart of Jesus Sancho de Guerra

By Patti Dansereau

St. Maria Josefa of the Heart of Jesus is a perfect example of what can happen when a soul totally abandons itself to God in complete trust and allows God to work in and through it for His glory. It wasn't St. Maria Josefa's accomplishments, but who she became that inspires the Church to hold her up as an example.

Maria Josefa was born on September 7, 1842 in Vitoria, Spain, to Bernabe Sancho and Petra de Guerra. The first Carlist war had just ended, in which Isabella II defeated her uncle, Charles V, for the throne. Thus, there was great political unrest and a growing liberalism and animosity toward the Church. Despite this, Maria Josefa grew up in a deeply Christian home, rich in virtue but poor in material comforts. Her father made rattan chairs to support his family. He passed away from a brain hemorrhage in 1850 at the age of 32 when Maria Josefa was only seven.

Although she could not express it in words at the time, from a very young age she felt a calling from God deep within her to help His people. She was an average youth except for her love and devotion to the Eucharist and the Blessed Virgin Mary.

Maria Josefa was very close to her mother. Despite their closeness Petra de Guerra fully supported and encouraged her daughter's call to the religious life. Maria Josefa once said, "Nobody beats me when it comes to loving their parents; however I made the sacrifice once and for always, leaving home was as if I had died."

While she knew she had a calling, Maria Josefa was not sure where to go. She had the choice of a cloistered order or an institute that was active in the surrounding community. Because she loved solitude she felt a cloistered order was where she was meant to be. After meeting Fr. Mariano Estarta, Delegate of the General of the Franciscans in Spain, and sharing with him what she wanted, he guided her towards the nuns of the Immaculate Conception in Aranjuez. When it came time for her to leave, she became extremely sick with typhus and had to cancel her trip.

When she was well again, Maria Josefa felt led by the Lord to go to Madrid where she asked to join the new order the Handmaids of Mary Serving the Sick (also known as the Servants of Mary) on December 3, 1864. The order was founded by St. Maria Soledad Torres Acosta. Its mission was to visit the sick in their homes, especially at night.

On December 25, 1864 Maria Josefa was given the religious habit and she took the name Sister Maria of Health. She was eager to abandon herself totally to the Lord and follow Him no matter where He led her.

During the 1865 cholera epidemic, she worked in the poorest areas of Madrid attending the sick. It was during this time that she met St. Antonio Maria Claret who was able to help her with her doubts that she was where the Lord wanted her to be. St. Antonio prayed about it and felt that God wanted her to take her temporal vows with the Servants of Mary, which she then did on January 1, 1866.

Over the next few years, although she was very busy helping the sick and knew it was her calling, Sister Maria of Health realized that the Servants of Mary was lacking something she needed - community life. After consulting her superiors, and with their approval, she left the order in July 1871. Despite the political unrest, she placed herself under the protection of the Blessed Virgin, to whom she was deeply devoted, and moved to Bilbao in northern Spain with two other community members. There she co-founded the Institute of the Servants of Jesus. Their mission was to minister to the sick in their homes at night, attend to patients in hospitals and clinics, help the elderly in their residences, and care for abandoned infants and children in day care centers.

In August, Maria Josefa and Mother Sacramento went to Vitoria with a draft of their constitution to obtain the local bishop's permission to work in his diocese. The bishop granted probationary permission and asked them to refine their constitution. To be an official order they also needed five members.

The three women began their work with eagerness and diligence. They were without money at first, so Maria Josefa's two companions worked to raise funds while Maria Josefa tended to the sick and saw to the sisters' spiritual exercises. The community life she had envisioned started to take shape. Together, they cared for the sick, prayed and shared in community. During that first year, two more members of the Servants of Mary joined them and they had to move from their little apartment on Esperanza Street to a bigger one on Ronda Street. Now they had their five members to become an official order.

The sisters faced and endured great sacrifices for the love of God and the salvation of the sick. But in 1873, they were called to heroic measures when Bilbao was ravaged by the Second Carlist war, another fight for the throne of Spain. They had to leave their apartment and move into the Convent of the Conception on the outskirts of Bilbao until the siege on the city was over. But the danger and cannon fire did not stop Maria Josefa and her companions from continuing their care of the sick, including the wounded from the war. Maria Josefa had put her complete trust in the

Sacred Heart of Jesus for their protection and knew that if He wanted the institute to expand and spread His love throughout the world, He would accomplish it in His way.

In 1874, when Bilbao was freed from the siege but the war still ravaged on, Maria Josefa and Mother Sacramento went to Vitoria on foot disguised as peasants to present to the Bishop their revised constitution. The following month, the Bishop gave the institute his approval. Not long after, the Servants of Jesus conducted its first vote and elected Maria Josefa of the Heart of Jesus as Superior, a position she held until her death. They received their final Decree of Approval from His Holiness Pope Leo XIII on January 8, 1886.

Maria Josefa's ideals for the Institute are spelled out in their first three articles:

1. The general aim of the Institute of the Servants of Jesus is to sanctify its members, through the practice of the three vows of poverty, chastity and obedience and the exact observance of these Constitutions.
2. The special aim is to take care of the sick in their homes and in hospitals, orphaned children in public establishments and other welfare and charity work.
3. However this material work is only a means by which to reach a spiritual aim consisting of the sanctification of the sick, children, the needy and anyone else with them.

Once the Institute was approved and they began receiving novices in 1875, the Servants started to expand at a rate only God could foresee. For the next 37 years Maria Josefa continued to give herself completely to the Lord as she strove unceasingly for the expansion of the Institute to bring the love of Jesus and the Good News of salvation to the sick.

From 1875 - 1885 Maria Josefa served in three positions: superior general, local superior and novice mistress. In accordance with the constitution, she taught the young novices how to love and take care of the sick in their physical and spiritual needs and guided them along their path to 'religious perfection'. She constantly urged her novices to "be souls of prayer" which was her own motto. But most important of all, through words and example she taught them to, "Always see the person of Jesus Christ in the patient."

In abandoning herself to God, He was able to equip her for the difficult task of leadership. He gave her the gifts she needed to fulfill her role as novice mistress and superior. She had a deep motherly love for all the sisters in her community and wanted them all to be happy. She was constantly worried that their needs were being met and tried to please them as best she could. She even made sure that they did not forget their own families. "The nun who does not love her own parents cannot love religion or her superiors."

But Maria Josefa also knew their need to grow in holiness. She had an ability to treat each one as a unique individual and took great pains to guide each novice along the path that God was calling her. God also gave her a special gift of being able to see past exteriors to what was really happening in their hearts. She once said, "I can see them all so clearly, I wish I couldn't see so much." The Spirit of God shone through her demeanor. Through a simple look or word of encouragement she was able to bring peace to the troubled and calm the worst interior storms in her sisters.

As the number of Servants grew, so did Maria Josefa's vision for the Institute. Under her care and guidance, the Servants of Jesus became well known and loved by the people of Spain and their services were always in high demand. Maria Josefa worked out of the mother-house in Bilbao and traveled extensively and opened 42 new foundations in other cities, starting with Castro Urdiales where the sisters were asked to take over the hospital. With pleas for help from Bishops and lay people, foundations opened in Valladolid, Burgos, Vitoria and many others. The last foundation that opened during Maria Josefa's lifetime was in Chile, but she could not go there herself, as she was too sick.

The Servants had a formula that worked for them. They were not afraid to live in poverty and hardship. Because serving the sick was their mission, they used whatever available housing best suited their needs, usually a small apartment or house. They sacrificed and prayed until they were able to afford or were donated a house of their own. In every case, the Lord supplied the Servants with homes within a few years of starting their work in the different cities.

Maria Josefa of the Heart of Jesus governed the growing Institute with great patience, humility and kindness. "We never ever saw her give orders haughtily or arrogantly," one of the sisters said. "All her orders showed excellent skills of governing for the easy and quiet way in which she did it, even when she had to overcome great difficulties. She had a strength of mind with which she set out at times to do not only one but several things at the same time."

She knew the secret of being a good leader. "Our Mother knew only too well that if the Superiors won the hearts of their subjects with sweetness and affection, they would be able to dominate even understanding, therefore making peaceful perfection in the Institute," one of the sisters said. When she encountered troubles within her order her wisdom was, "Peace and unity demand that we suffer each other and we treat each other reciprocally with sweetness. Work to have an obedient heart, gentle, generous and condescending for the love of God. We must arm ourselves with strength but not to conquer our peers but to conquer ourselves."

Maria Josefa's gifted ability to run the Institute did not go unnoticed. In 1894, when it came time for her to step down from her position as superior general, Cardinal Archbishop Seville petitioned the Holy See to override the Servants of Jesus' constitution and keep her as superior general without the need for her to be re-elected. He had the backing of the other bishops who had the Servants working in their diocese. The Holy See agreed and ordered her to remain superior indefinitely. Her response was: "I never stopped to think of it as an honor or distinction but rather another heavy cross that the Lord was putting on my weak shoulders. Because of its great weight and nature it tore sorrowful cries from my heart and bitter tears from my eyes." Maria Josefa suffered the weight of her new cross in silence. The Document of the Sacred Congregation was only made public two months before her death.

It was not what Maria Josefa of the Heart of Jesus accomplished that made her a saint, except in the sense that everything she did was done with humility and total surrender to God. The way she lived her life can be summed up in the first two commandments; she loved the Lord her God with all her mind, heart, soul and strength, and loved her neighbor as herself. In her great love for God and neighbor, she longed for everyone to live the same way. That desire was lived out in her care that the Institute expand and that all the Servants of Jesus reached spiritual and professional perfection.

Maria Josefa's own devotion to the Heart of Jesus allowed Him to form her heart after His own and as a result she grew in love and kindness for everyone. One of her sisters once wrote about her, "I admired her great humility and gentleness and the low concept she had of herself; she didn't want to be talked about. In everything that had no direct relation to her position she was the first to give away. What characterized our Mother most was the way in which she wanted to live hidden and forgotten, unknown to the world. She used to say with exemplar humility, that if she was known, she would lose the Institute."

She suggested that the Servants follow her example and take the Sacred Heart as their role model: "Let us imitate its profound humility, its love of sacrifice and zeal for the salvation of souls. Without forgetting charity, which should start with ourselves by helping each other and bearing each other's defects and encouraging each other by setting a good example in advancing in perfection."

Even with all the demands of running the Institute, Maria Josefa never lost sight of her own journey back to her Father's house. It took her down a path most people would rather avoid, but which she walked with great joy, as one sister attested to, "Our Reverend Mother had a living faith. She made it a standing part of her work and she obtained a great dislike of all earthly things and a high concept of eternal life. Through her faith she discovered hidden treasures in suffering."

Maria Josefa continually exhorted her sisters to embrace their own crosses and sufferings. "The important thing now is that you steadfastly embrace the cross that the Lord prepares for you, whatever is His divine will. If He wants to lead you along the path of the cross and sacrifice, I understand and it is only natural that one resists, but once you begin to walk confidently along this way, you will not be able to leave it. As you will see, it is the one that leads us to the real purpose more quickly." "Heaven is conquered by pain. Whenever you find yourself alone, abandoned, burdened with grief, crowned with thorns, weighed down by chains and held up on the cross, lift your head and smile at your God, because these tortures are a pledge to eternal happiness."

"Take heart and generously offer the pains of your suffering to the Lord and consider that the most precious cross, where souls are purified, is in illness."

Her own physical suffering took the form of a heart condition that kept her in constant pain and prevented her from sleeping. In 1901, she was stricken with paralysis, which she recovered from only temporarily. The way she responded to her illness was the way she lived her live, in total surrender. "I'm packing my little case for my journey to eternity. I don't want to go without the virtues of a religious soul and the first to be packed are poverty and humility."

Her ultimate focus was on eternity. On one of her birthdays she was reported as saying, "It reminds me that I have a year less to live and I am nearer to eternity."

Closer to the end of her life, as if her weak heart wasn't enough suffering, she also had chronic bronchitis. During her last days she suffered terribly from bronchi-pneumonia, but even with the paralysis of her throat and bronchial tubes she received and was able to swallow her final Eucharist moments before her death. On March 20, 1921, at age 79, she peacefully surrendered her soul to her beloved Lord Jesus.

Initially she was buried in Derio Cemetery, in Bilbao. On January 2, 1926, her body was discovered in an uncorrupted state. January 15, she was moved to her final resting-place at the mother-house on Naja Street. Her presence there is a reminder to the Servants of Jesus today that God can live again on earth in our midst if we only let Him, just as St. Maria Josefa of the Heart of Jesus did.

Maria Josefa of the Heart of Jesus was declared venerable, on September 7, 1989, and beatified on September 27, 1992.

Even after her death, she continued to help the sick through her intercession. Many miracles are attributed to her intercession, but the miracle that caught Rome's attention and completed her canonization process took place in 1992 in Armenia, Quindio, Spain.

On August 11, Juan Carlos Ospina Bolanos was born thirteen weeks premature weighing less than two pounds and had severely underdeveloped lungs. The child's mother requested prayers. Mother Isabel Gonzalez Arnoso, the superior of the Central Clinic at the time, prayed a novena to Blessed Maria Josefa and placed one of her relics in the baby's incubator. In time, the tiny baby grasped the medal in his little hand. The boy's parents were encouraged to pray the novena as well which they did.

On August 14, Juan Carlos suffered a heart attack that lasted seven to eight minutes. He suffered three more between Aug. 22 and 24. After his fourth heart attack, the doctors believed there was nothing more they could do to save him and recommended to the family that no more extreme measures be taken to save his life. From that day on Juan Carlos only received the minimal necessary treatment.

Juan Carlos made a complete recovery. Dr. Palacio, Juan Carlos' pediatrician, went to Rome to testify to the miracle of the child's recovery. "I cannot erase from my memory the moment at which I was with the boy and he took in his little hand the image of the Beatified Maria Josefa of the Heart of Jesus. And from that moment on, the Sisters did not doubt for a minute in the improvement of the boy. While they involved the family of the patient in their orations, and their optimism and security increased, mine from the medical point of view every minute diminished. If you requested me to say what happened, in a word, only one could summarize it: Miracle."

On June 28, 1999, Pope John Paul II approved the miracle. Maria Josefa of the Heart of Jesus was then canonized on October 1, 2000.

Today, her daughters continue her work and her love for Jesus in the sick in 93 houses found not only in Spain and Chile but in Mexico, the Dominican Republic, Peru, Ecuador, Columbia, Argentina, Philippians, Paraguay, Portugal, Italy and France.

Patti Dansereau originates from Canada, but lives in Bismarck ND with her husband and three children. When she isn't in the garden pulling weeds and pruning bushes, she loves to write children's chapter books that will encourage children to have a personal relationship with Jesus. Her non-fiction work appears in Parent Care.

Tim Drake

References

"Canonizacion." May 29, 2000. *Instituto de las Siervas de Jesus de la Caridad.* http://www.siervasdejesus.com/canonizacion.htm

"El Milagro." May 29, 2000. *Instituto de las Siervas de Jesus de la Caridad.* http://www.siervasdejesus.com/milagro.htm

"125 Aniversario de Fundacion del Instituto de las Siervas de Jesus de la Caridad." *Instituto De Las Siervas de Jesus de la Caridad.* http://www.siervasdejesus.com/aniversa.htm (April 1, 2000).

Pablo Bilbao Aristegui, *Saint Maria Josefa del Corazon de Jesus.* (Bilbao, Spain: Ediciones Mensajero, 2000)

"Semblanzas de la Beata Maria Josefa del Corazon de Jesus Fundadora del Instituto Siervas de Jesus." *Instituto de las Siervas de Jesus de la Caridad.*

http://www.siervasdejesus.com/semblanz.htm (April 1, 2000).

Website "El Milagro"

Tim Drake

St. Katharine Drexel

By Tom Kreitzberg

On October 1, 2000, Katharine Drexel became a saint for the Universal Church, yet her story will always be distinctively American. The daughter of a self-made millionaire, she used her inheritance to salve the two great wounds of her country in ministering to the African American and American Indian peoples.

Katharine was born in Philadelphia on November 26, 1858, the second daughter of Francis and Hannah Drexel. By this time, the 34-year-old Francis was a nationally known banker, who with his brother Anthony had turned Drexel and Company into one of the country's leading investment firms.

It was a difficult birth, and Hannah never recovered. When she died five weeks later, Francis arranged for the infant Katharine and her three-year-old sister Elizabeth to stay with their Uncle Anthony and Aunt Ellen, who cared for them during Francis's time of mourning.

In April 1860, Francis married Emma Bouvier, and Elizabeth and Katharine joined them in their new home. Emma Drexel was a true mother to Lizzie and Katie, even after her own daughter Louise was born in 1863. Katie didn't even realize Emma wasn't her natural mother until she noticed she had more grandmothers than she had parents. Emma saw to it that Hannah's daughters paid weekly visits to their maternal grandmother, Eliza Langstroth. A Protestant, Eliza taught her granddaughters by example that Catholics were not the only Christians capable of pious and sincere faith.

The houses of American millionaires are not often thought of as incubators of sanctity. But then, the marriage of Francis and Emma Drexel was not what might be expected between a wealthy widower and a rich younger woman. They were both ardent Catholics, and they saw in their marriage an opportunity to help each other grow in faith. Emma had a small oratory built in their house, where night prayers were said as a family. "Prayer was like breathing," Katharine once said of life in the Drexel home.

While Francis preferred to pray where the servants wouldn't see him, Emma carried out a highly visible apostolate. Three times a week, she received the poor of Philadelphia at the back door of her house. She listened to the stories of hungry children, bare feet, and cold apartments, and she helped out as she could. Over time, this evolved into a systematic private charity, complete with a paid assistant.

The example of her parents had a profound effect on young Katie, who was naturally inclined to generosity and love of God. But though she was an exceptionally selfless child, she was still a child, and not above throwing the occasional public tantrum to get what she wanted. (Her mother, alas, wasn't one to be shamed into giving in to such tactics). Katie was also fond of the finer things in a girl's life. Emma had her daughters' dresses made at a nearby convent, and Katie once begged the sister who measured her to add lots of lace and ruffles. In a writing assignment from her tutor, she asked her mother, "Will you have my ears pierced soon, for I am in such a hurry to have my ears pierced? Everybody loves earrings."

In 1870, the Drexels bought and renovated a farm in the Philadelphia suburb of Torresdale. They named their country home St. Michael, and here the Drexel girls spent many happy days. Emma established a Sunday school for the children of the neighborhood, and installed Lizzie and Kate as the instructors. At one time, as many as fifty students attended, and the school remained active until 1888.

Katharine's love of God continued to deepen during her time at St. Michael. She was a frequent communicant at the chapel of a nearby convent school, and one day the students were told that she had fainted after Mass. It turned out that, on arriving at the chapel, Katherine fell from her horse and broke her collarbone. Determined to receive Communion, she said nothing of her pain until Mass was finished.

The purchase of St. Michael turned out to have another benefit no one could have predicted. In 1872, a priest named James O'Connor was appointed pastor of St. Dominic's parish, which included St. Michael. The ties he established with the Drexel family, and particularly with Katharine, were to last until his death, and as Katharine's spiritual director gave permanent shape to her vocation.

While the family's thoughts were never long away from God, it remains true that the Drexels were tremendously wealthy, and even taking into account the girls' willing self-sacrifices, there was nothing they wanted that they could not have. Private tutors, vacations at Cape May and Newport, an eight-month tour of Europe: these were the practical benefits of the Drexel brothers' success. The diary Katharine kept as an eighteen-year-old is that of a playful, intelligent young woman of the world; unlike her patron, St. Catherine of Siena, she was not at that age withdrawn into a cell the better to know and love Christ.

But she kept other journals, which she called her "accounts," in which she attempted to track her spiritual development according to the program of the well-known spiritual writer, Father Frederick William Faber. As early as 1874, when she was fifteen, her primary New Year's resolution was "To overcome Pride and Vanity," and the same year she vowed to give up butter, fruit, and between-meal snacks for Lent. More than four years later, in May 1878, she was continuing to read Father Faber, but wrote, "I have done scarcely anything to correct pride and vanity." While the pride of a saint may not be noticeable in the world, and Fr. O'Connor warned Katharine that her predominant passion was scrupulosity, her private accounts as she approached adulthood show her to be one who failed every time she attempted to perfect herself. As importantly, they also show her to be one who tried again after every failure.

There was a curious tension, as well, between being the daughter of the wealthy banker Francis Drexel and being the daughter of the reserved philanthropist Emma Drexel. Katharine was expected and encouraged to go out into society (not the very best society, of course; the Drexels were Catholic and didn't inherit their money). At the same time, she and her sisters knew that, to the extent they lived in the world, they would have to live apart from their mother. Emma was a dutiful wife and hostess, but her heart was in the work she did for the poor. Time spent socializing was time spent not serving. With such a mother, who can wonder if Katharine often felt a failure in her spiritual life, and as often felt inspired to continue to try?

Katharine finished her formal schooling in July 1878, and the following January, shortly after her twentieth birthday, she made her social debut. All that was required of her was to enjoy a life of leisure until she obtained a suitable husband and settled down. But, despite the encouragement of her parents — somewhat more restrained, perhaps, on the part of her father — Katharine passed her first few years in society without entanglement.

During this time, her mother grew increasingly ill. Emma tried to conceal her pain and weakness from the family, but when a diagnosis of cancer was announced, Katharine determined to be her constant companion. She sat by her mother's bedside and agonized over her suffering. As she nursed her mother through spasms of pain, Katharine began to seriously consider a religious vocation.

After a brave, painful struggle, Emma Drexel died on January 29, 1883. It was a loss felt as much by the poor as by those in her own social class. She had given away half a million dollars during her marriage and was paying the rent for 150 families at the time of her death.

Following Emma's death, Katharine wrote to James O'Connor, now bishop of Omaha, and told him of her growing interest in becoming a nun. Bishop O'Connor's advice was, "Think, pray, wait." The child of privilege would practice some acts of self-denial and focus on her interior life, but at this point her advisor believed she was destined to live as an example to the secular world.

In October 1883, Francis and his daughters began an extended tour of Europe, to take their minds off their grief. During this trip, Katharine followed Bishop O'Connor's advice and limited herself to an hour and a half of prayers each day. She also made a vow of virginity, binding for one year, before a much-venerated painting of the Virgin Mary in Venice. This, too, was on the advice of the bishop, although she found it contrary to her desire to settle on the religious life right away.

Shortly after the Drexel family returned to Philadelphia in May 1884, Francis announced that he had made his will in such a way as to protect his daughters from treasure hunters. The banker was quite pleased with himself, although of course his daughters were alarmed at the suggestion of his mortality.

It was a suggestion that would come to pass quite unexpectedly. While recovering from a mild case of pleurisy, Francis died suddenly on February 15, 1885. The three sisters — all in their twenties, all unmarried, all heirs to a banking fortune — were orphaned.

Francis's will caused a stir throughout the country. One tenth of his estate was to be paid out to a variety of charities. The remaining nine-tenths, $14,000,000, was to be invested, with the annual income paid out in equal shares to his daughters. Should one die without leaving children, the surviving women would then split the income. Should all three die without children, the remaining assets would be distributed among the charities named in his will.

Elizabeth, Katharine, and Louise were all determined to continue the tradition of charity their parents had handed on to them. Living together in their childhood home, they each took special interest in a different apostolate. Elizabeth followed in her father's footsteps by funding the construction of a trade school for older boys from the Philadelphia orphanages Francis had supported. Louise, meanwhile, concentrated her attention on helping poor black Americans. Katharine found herself drawn to support missions to the Indians of the American West, thanks in part to a meeting with Fr. Joseph Stephan, director of the Bureau of Catholic Indian Missions. Bishop O'Connor had recommended Fr. Stephan ask for her help in funding missions, and Katharine responded with characteristic enthusiasm and generoslty.

Francis's death had hit Katharine hard. By the summer of 1886, her health deteriorated to the point where her doctor advised her to take the cure at a German health spa. She agreed, and with her sisters sailed for Europe once more.

Katharine soon recovered her health, and the Drexels began a leisurely tour of Europe. In January 1887, they obtained a private audience with Pope Leo XIII. Katharine used the opportunity to tell the Pope of the great need for missionary priests among the Indians of Wyoming. The Pope said to her, "Why not, my child, yourself become a missionary?"

Katharine answered, "Because, Holy Father, sisters can be had for the missions, but no priests."

This exchange left Katharine feeling frightened and sick, and as soon as she left the Vatican she began sobbing. Her idea of a vocation, still far from settled with Bishop O'Connor, was as a contemplative. The Pope's simple suggestion had opened up a vertiginous new window on the future, and she was not yet ready to look upon all that being a missionary would demand of her.

The Drexel sisters returned to Philadelphia in the spring of 1887, but by September they were traveling once more. This time, they were touring the Indian missions with Bishop O'Connor and Fr. Stephan. It was a rough trip, much of it made by horse-drawn wagon, but they knew the importance of understanding the hardships faced by the Indians and those who served them. Kate dedicated herself to building the schools that were so desperately needed, all the while struggling with the question of her own destiny.

Why was Bishop O'Connor so resistant to the idea of Kate entering a convent? There were several reasons. Kate herself had admitted she feared community life would be trying, and she wasn't sure that she could place herself under obedience to a superior whom she found stupid. For a time her health was too poor. Beyond that, some of her letters suggested that she wanted to become a nun because it was a higher calling, not because it was her own calling. Finally, as he wrote to her in May 1888, her good works "give more glory to God, and do your neighbor more good, than anything you could accomplish in a religious community."

At last, though, in November 1888, Katharine wrote to Bishop O'Connor: "Are you afraid to give me to Jesus Christ?... It appears to me, Reverend Father, that I am not obliged to *submit* my judgment to yours, as I have been doing for two years, for I feel so sad in doing it, because the world cannot give me peace, so restless because my heart is not rested in God."

Within days, she received his reply. "This letter of yours," he wrote, "and your bearing under the long and severe tests to which I subjected you, as well as your entire restoration to health, and the many spiritual dangers that surround you, make me withdraw all opposition to your entering religion... The only matter that, now, remains to be determined is, which order should you choose?"

As if this instantaneous reversal of five years' opposition to Katharine's religious vocation weren't a sharp enough change, less than three months later Bishop O'Connor wrote to her with a grand new vision. "The more I have thought of your case the more convinced I become that God has called you to establish an order for [the Indian and Colored people]."

This was an idea that terrified Katharine. It was now the bishop's turn to convince his spiritual daughter of the true nature of her vocation. They exchanged a flurry of letters, with Katharine raising objection after objection — she wished to be a contemplative and to receive Communion daily; she doubted her ability to provide a fitting example as founder; a new order would face various delays and oppositions that an old order would not; perhaps all the orders should help in the work. Bishop O'Connor countered each of her objections and persisted in his conviction. On March 19, 1889, she gave in, writing to him, "The Feast of St. Joseph brought me the grace...to enter fully and entirely into your views...."

The next month, Katharine and Elizabeth paid a visit to the Sisters of Mercy mother-house in Pittsburgh, where Bishop O'Connor thought Katharine could best prepare herself for religious life. (Louise was unavailable to join her sisters, since she had married Edward Morrell in January.) Katharine agreed with Bishop O'Connor's opinion of the Sisters of Mercy, and on May 7, 1889, she became a postulant in their mother-house. Here she intended to learn all she could about the religious life, until the time came for her to make her vows as the first member and superior of her own order. The lessons taught by the novice mistress, though, were far from the hardest she would learn during her time in Pittsburgh.

Bishop O'Connor fell ill a few months after Katharine entered the postulancy. Despite the best efforts of his doctors, and of Katharine herself, who helped bring him to a Pittsburgh hospital and nursed him for some weeks, he died on May 27, 1890. The man who had served and advised Katharine for half her life, the one whose vision of her life she had agreed to live, was taken from her.

Katharine was devastated. When Archbishop Patrick J. Ryan of Philadelphia visited her after Bishop O'Connor's Requiem Mass, she told him that she could not go through with the plan. He asked her, "If I share the burden with you, if I help you, can you go on?" From that day until his death in 1911, Archbishop Ryan was Katharine's constant supporter and champion.

This was not the end of her personal sorrows for 1890. Her sister Elizabeth, who married Walter George Smith at the beginning of the year, fell ill during their honeymoon in Europe. They returned to Philadelphia in early September, with Elizabeth not fully recovered but expecting a child. Later that month, she went into premature labor and died; her child was stillborn.

What passed between Katharine and her Lord as she struggled to accept these losses remained, for the most part, within her heart. In faith and hope, she survived her trials and continued to prepare for her profession of vows and the birth of her congregation.

Public announcement of her intent to found an order dedicated to caring for Indians and African-Americans had been made following her formal reception into religious life on November 7, 1889. As a novice with the Sisters of Mercy, Sister Katharine had the added duty of interviewing and accepting candidates for her own order. The candidates, who grew to thirteen in number, joined her in the novitiate in Pittsburgh.

The question of what to do with Katharine's inheritance needed to be settled. Katharine, who had been a Third Order Franciscan, wanted to give it all away and let her order embrace poverty from its foundation. In the end, though, she agreed to use her thousand dollars a day income to help establish her order, with the understanding that, following her death, it would rely on donations from the Catholic faithful.

On February 12, 1891, before Archbishop Ryan and a small group of family and friends, Katharine vowed "poverty, chastity, and obedience and to be the mother and servant of the Indians and colored people," becoming Mother Mary Katharine Drexel of the Sisters of the Blessed Sacrament for Indians and Colored Peoples. Soon afterwards, she and her group of novices — together with two Sisters of Mercy assigned to help them — left Pittsburgh for her family home of St. Michael, where they planned on staying until construction of the order's mother-house in what is now Bensalem, Pennsylvania, was completed.

As it turned out, they couldn't wait quite that long. The community moved into its mother-house, St. Elizabeth's Convent, on December 3, 1892, several months after construction was to have been finished but a couple of months before it actually was. This pattern, of expectations, setbacks and impatience, would become familiar to the members of the young order. They were eager to be sent to the missions; Mother Katharine had even surveyed (and helped pay for the construction of) the ideal spot for them to begin, St. Stephen's Mission in Wyoming.

Archbishop Ryan, however, was not so eager to rush the new sisters into the field. It wasn't until June 1894, that he allowed the first Sisters of the Blessed Sacrament to depart the mother-house for mission work. Their destination was St. Catherine's School, in Santa Fe, New Mexico. Named in honor of Mother Katharine, who had funded its construction in 1886, the school had been closed in 1893 due to lack of personnel. Nine Blessed Sacrament sisters were sent to staff the school, equaling the number of students enrolled when it opened in September 1894. More students would arrive, however, and the Sisters of the Blessed Sacrament operated the school until it closed in 1999.

At the same time she was sending out her first missionaries to serve Indians, Mother Katharine was looking to involve her congregation in work with African Americans. After getting support for her plans from the bishop of Richmond, she bought a 600-acre farm in Rock Castle, Virginia, adjacent to a 1,600-acre estate her sister Louise had purchased. While Louise established the St. Emma's Industrial and Agricultural Institute, a school for black boys, Mother Katharine oversaw construction of the St. Francis de Sales High School for black girls. As always, she directed this project with a diligence and attention to detail that would have made her banker father proud.

St. Francis de Sales opened in October 1899, though not before someone had set fire to the barn just before the sisters from St. Elizabeth's Convent arrived in July. This was neither the first nor last time the Sisters of the Blessed Sacrament would embark on a project in the face of deep-seated ill will.

The work of the congregation in the Diocese of Richmond extended beyond St. Francis's school grounds. In addition to going out into the community to help the poor directly, the sisters soon began a forty-year-long apostolate to nearby prisons. Mother Katharine's chance discovery of a private Catholic chapel along the train route to Lynchburg led to the formation of a Sunday school in Columbia, Virginia.

One of Mother Katharine's most challenging goals was the establishment of a mission to the Navajos in Arizona. In 1896, she had purchased land for the mission, but was immediately faced with the usual problem of finding priests to work there. In October 1898, three Franciscan priests arrived, eager to help Mother Katharine realize her dream. With their assistance, particularly their groundbreaking efforts to learn the notoriously difficult Navajo language, Mother Katharine was able to open St. Michael's School in 1902.

The next major undertaking for the Sisters of the Blessed Sacrament was Immaculate Conception Academy, a school for black girls in Nashville, Tennessee. In 1905, when Mother Katharine purchased the property for the academy, Nashville was not a city that welcomed the idea of Catholics teaching blacks in a white neighborhood. The bishop of Nashville, Thomas Byrne, arranged for a third party to buy the property, after Mother Katharine settled for a quick look at it from a closed carriage.

All in all, that was a memorable day for Mother Katharine and her traveling companion, Mother Mary Mercedes. It was the eve of the Feast of the Purification, one of the congregation's fast days. Due to a late train the day before and an unexpected snowstorm, they returned for supper to the Dominican convent where they were staying without having eaten a full meal in more than thirty hours. Thinking they had had a large dinner that afternoon with Bishop Byrne, and knowing that it was a fast day for them, the Dominican sister caring for them served them a little bread, tea, and cake. Mother Mercedes, in her account of this trip, wrote, "For the first time in years, Mother Katharine consumed two pieces of cake!"

When the man who sold Mother Katharine the property for their academy learned what it would be used for, he attempted first to buy it back, then to bribe Bishop Byrne into getting another order to take over the property, and finally to have the city run a street directly through the property. All of his attempts came to nothing, and the school opened in September 1905. By the end of the school year, the original building was too small for the enrollment, and a larger school had to be built. Immaculate Conception Academy continued to thrive until 1954, when the schools of Nashville were integrated and the academy was closed.

Establishing new missions for her spiritual daughters was not all that Mother Katharine was doing at this time. In addition to her duties as Mother General, she was Mistress of Novices for the congregation, and she still had her inheritance to disburse — with great liberality yet great care — among all the Indian and black missions that sought her assistance. She was also occupied with getting Vatican approval for the rule for her community. Work on this began in 1894 and continued until 1907. Shortly before Mother Katharine was ready to send the final version of the rule to Rome, she received a surprise visitor to St. Elizabeth's Convent, Mother Cabrini of the Missionary Sisters of the Sacred Heart of Jesus. Mother Cabrini advised her, "If you want to get your Rule approved, you go yourself to Rome and take it with you."

When Mother Katharine arrived in Rome in May, 1907, Monsignor Richard Kennedy of the American College told her the priest who was to help her translate the rule into ecclesial Latin had died and there was no one else available at the time. Distraught, she went to the Minerva and prayed for assistance at the tomb of St. Catherine of Siena. Two days later, Monsignor Kennedy informed her that he had dined the day before with a priest from Philadelphia who had just finished preparing the constitution of the Philadelphia Franciscans. This priest, Fr. Joseph Schwarz, C.SS.R., agreed to help, and within three weeks he and a translator he procured were providing the printer with pages of the rule as fast as they could be printed. Less than two months after she arrived, Mother Katharine left Rome with her rule approved by the Pope for a trial period of five years.

1912 was a busy year for the 53-year-old Mother General. In addition to all her other duties, Mother Katharine was personally involved in arrangements for opening missions in Columbus, New York City, and Chicago. For her, involvement meant trudging through Harlem in the heat of summer looking for suitable housing, and working from morning till night helping to clean and prepare the new convents. During a visitation of St. Catherine's in Santa Fe, however, she contracted typhoid and was forced to rest at the Albuquerque Sanitarium. After the doctor told her his diagnosis, she settled back in bed and said, "Well, I feel perfect peace on an occasion like this, as this is certainly not according to my plans, and it must be God's Will."

Naturally, the entire Community was alarmed at the news, the more so because she insisted that no one from the mother-house come to visit her. She even forbade her sister Louise from coming. As a result, Louise's husband, Edward Morrell, arrived in Albuquerque and took charge of his sister-in-law. He arranged for her nursing, insisted on certain medical tests, and paid for a private train car to take her back to Philadelphia by a low-altitude route. Mother Katharine recovered, and was well enough to travel to Rome in the spring of 1913 for the final approbation of the congregation's rule.

Although Louisiana had a large population of black Catholics, the Sisters of the Blessed Sacrament did not open a mission there for many years. Mother Katharine did not want to do anything that would hurt the Sisters of the Holy Family, a black congregation centered in New Orleans. In 1915, however, the Archbishop of New Orleans asked her to open a school there that might develop into a college. This was a task that was too large for the Sisters of the Holy Family to undertake, and Mother Katharine eagerly accepted the invitation. Xavier Academy opened in September 1915. It continues today as Xavier University, the only historically black Catholic college in the United States.

These are the tasks with which Mother Katharine Drexel occupied herself, but with what spirit? Of central importance, in her own life and in the life of her congregation, was the Holy Eucharist. She obtained for the mother-house the right to daily exposition and adoration, simply by asking Archbishop Prendergast of Philadelphia. Instead of the refusal she had expected, he replied, "Why, have you not got it? I thought you had."

Mother Katharine once explained what prayer before the Blessed Sacrament offers: "The religious needs strength. Near the tabernacle the soul finds strength, consolation, and resignation. The religious needs virtue. Jesus is the model of virtues in the Blessed Sacrament. The religious needs hope. In the Blessed Sacrament we possess the most precious pledge of our hope."

For Mother Katharine, the Eucharist was a testament of Jesus' boundless love in the sacrifice of the Cross. This was a sacrifice she struggled to perfect in herself, in accepting the sorrows that came to her and in emptying herself of anything that did not give glory to God and serve the poor. She often remained in the chapel after the other sisters left, kneeling before the crucifix, tears streaming down her face as she meditated on the Crucifixion. "There is no other way to heaven," she wrote. "No one's face is toward heaven when it is not toward Calvary."

Another feature of her spirituality was a radical embrace of holy poverty. It was not mere frugality that led her to reuse envelopes she received for memo paper, to bring her own food for train rides, to be vigilant against wasting water and electricity. She lived the Franciscan ideal of poverty as a way to draw close to Jesus, Who, in her words, "lived poor, died poor, and the last treasure He gave away was His mother."

"If you are to keep the congregation in existence," she once wrote, "poverty must be its first entrenchment. One single man, Francis, sustained the wall of the Church — through extreme poverty. All saints lived poor lives. The Sister unfaithful to poverty is an enemy of her congregation."

But Mother Katharine was a saint, and it is very difficult to be a gloomy saint. Her letters to St. Elizabeth's, written during her visitations of the missions, show the same sense of humor and wonder that she had as a young woman writing home from her European tours. In person, she was engaging, filled with energy and enthusiasm for whatever lay before her, and above all joyful. One sister later recalled how, when as a postulant in 1926 she waited to meet the Mother General, her vision of a tall, austere woman was shattered when the real Mother General arrived at the mother-house, looked at her, and said, "Oh, a new postulant. Goody, goody, goody."

This was the spirit needed to sustain the Sisters of the Blessed Sacrament in their work. To the countless challenges of the apostolate itself was often added the raw prejudice of local white people. Nashville was far from the only place in America where the idea of Catholics helping blacks and Indians was greeted with hatred. This hatred was directed against the congregation from its earliest days, when rumors were spread of planned violence during the laying of the mother-house's cornerstone.

The life of Mother Katharine, and that of her congregation, was to enter a new phase in 1935. After nearly forty-five years of constant toil, her health began to fail. She had a minor heart attack in Philadelphia, later a fainting spell on a visitation to St. Michael's Mission in Arizona, and finally a very serious heart attack in Chicago. Once transferred to a Philadelphia hospital, she was informed by her doctor that she must abandon her exhaustive schedule if she wanted to live.

Mother Katharine accepted this advice with equanimity. Her primary duties were transferred to her vicar, Mother Mercedes, who was formally elected the second Mother General of the Sisters of the Blessed Sacrament in 1937. Mother Katharine moved into the infirmary at the mother-house, her prayers and example continuing the work of instruction and guidance that her body was no longer capable of. Following Mother Mercedes's death in 1940, the last of Mother Katharine's administrative duties were transferred.

1941 marked the fiftieth anniversary of the Sisters of the Blessed Sacrament, and Catholic America made clear the esteem in which Mother Katharine was held. During a three-day celebration in April, cardinals and bishops joined graduates of the congregation's schools to honor the foundress. Cardinal Dougherty of Philadelphia called Mother Katharine "a shining glory, not only of Philadelphia, but also of our whole nation." Bishop Cushing of Boston wrote that she was "immortalized...in my memory and that of many others as the foremost individual benefactress of missionary work of the Catholic Church in North America." Pope Pius XII, too, sent a letter of congratulations and blessing.

The accolades did not end there. In 1939, the Catholic University of America had bestowed an honorary doctorate upon her, the first woman so honored by the university. In the jubilee year of 1941, Duquesne and Emmanuel College in Boston also conferred honorary doctorates on her, and St. Joseph's College in Philadelphia gave both her and her sister Louise honorary Doctor of Law degrees. The day after the ceremony at St. Joseph's, a sister stopped by Mother Katharine's room to say, "Our Mother is a doctor."

"Oh, I am a lot of doctors now!" she replied with a smile.

Mother Katharine spent her retirement in constant prayer and contemplation. It was the life the young Kate Drexel had hoped for, before Bishop O'Connor convinced her to found an active order. She wrote out her prayers on slips of paper, checking them off as she recited them. Twice a day, she prayed a fifteen-decade Rosary; she knew and recited many traditional litanies of the Church.

Her special love, though, continued to be Christ in the Blessed Sacrament. While her health permitted, she spent much of her time in view of the tabernacle in St. Elizabeth's chapel. She allowed herself one hour in the night for "nocturnal adoration" in her bed, though she often spent far more than that lost in meditation. Following a serious operation in 1943, she was given permission by Cardinal Dougherty to have Mass said in her room. The altar before which she had received her first Holy Communion was installed in her room, and she was able to assist at daily Mass for the rest of her life.

Mother Katharine recorded her meditations and intentions along with her prayers. As she called upon the mercy and love of God for others, she also sought an understanding of her own death in the light of the Eucharist. "Every activity," she wrote, "is a spiritual exercise preparing me for the coming of Christ — when He shall come to me at the hour of death."

In her attempt to unite herself perfectly to Jesus, Mother Katharine was both frank and critical towards her failings, just as she had been as a schoolgirl. One of her meditations reads, "It is hard to suffer patiently and lovingly. I offer it as a prayer for mercy for my innumerable sins and to obtain grace to do so through Mary, uniting my suffering to Our Lord in the host."

Louise Morrell died in 1943, a model to the end of the life Bishop O'Connor had once envisioned for Kate. As a Third Order Franciscan, Louise always treated her wealth as given to her to give to the poor. She came to visit her ailing sister every week, and her own unexpected death dealt Mother Katharine a cruel blow. But even as her tears fell, Mother Katharine struggled to accept the will of God: "It is not that I want anything different from what God wants... I cannot believe it."

Mother Katharine's own death came, after a night of troubled breathing, on March 3, 1955. Her casket was placed in St. Elizabeth's chapel for two days, while unexpected crowds of people filed past to catch a glimpse of the body of a saint. Her funeral Mass, at Philadelphia's Cathedral of Sts. Peter and Paul, was celebrated by Philadelphia Archbishop O'Hara, who was assisted by more than 250 bishops, priests, and brothers. The cathedral, where Katie Drexel had so often attended Mass as a child, was overflowing with people who had come for the funeral. Her body was interred in a crypt beneath the chapel of St. Elizabeth, where it remains as an object of veneration for the pilgrims attracted by her sanctity.

Following her death, the income with which she had supported the work of the Sisters of the Blessed Sacrament stopped. Under the terms of her father's will, the principal was divided among the charities Francis Drexel had identified in 1884. Mother Katharine had spent twenty million dollars on the poor over the years, while she herself lived a life of evangelical poverty.

The cause for her canonization was opened by Philadelphia Archbishop John Cardinal Krol in 1964. Through her intercession, a teenage boy named Roger Gutherman had his hearing restored in 1974, leading to her 1988 beatification. Hearing of Roger's story, the family of a deaf toddler named Amy Wells began praying to Bl. Katharine in 1993. Amy's miraculous cure cleared the way for Pope John Paul II to announce, on March 10, 2000, his approval of Bl. Katharine's canonization.

Tom Kreitzberg is a mathematician by training, a software developer by occupation, a Lay Dominican by profession, and a writer by night. His short stories, articles, and clerihews have appeared in a variety of publications, both in-print and on-line. He founded the Short Crime Fiction Review website and edits the Short Mystery Fiction Society's quarterly newsletter. He lives with his wife and children in suburban Maryland.

Tim Drake

Augustine Tchao and the Chinese Martyrs

By Christine Haapala with Fr. Matthew Carr

Among the Chinese martyrs, the Congregation for the Causes of Saints lists 120 martyred clergy, religious, laymen and laywomen that exemplify unwavering faith, sacrificial love, and unrelenting hope in the promise of eternal life. Each of these 120 "lights" burned brilliantly with the love of Christ's Church and the mission of evangelization but were extinguished by the hatred of a cruel people who could not bear to believe in the saving power of the Risen Christ. Each martyr lived powerfully the call to follow Christ and "to make disciples of all nations."

Individually, they are witnesses of the strength and endurance garnered from the grace of God and belief in truth, even to death. Collectively, they resound a formidable message of enduring and continuing response to God's call even under the hardest and cruelest of circumstances. They emerged gloriously, victorious from four bloody centuries of repression and are known as the Blessed Chinese Martyrs. Their feast day is celebrated by the Universal Church on September 28th.

17th – 18th Centuries
Martyrs of the Order of Preachers (Dominicans)
While the martyrdom of six Dominican preachers covered one hundred years (1648-1748), their Spanish heritage, devotion to the Most Holy Rosary, and fervent desire to evangelize China united them.

Father Francis Fernandez de Capillas dedicated himself to serving the mission fields of the Philippines for ten years and then preaching and baptizing for five years in the cities of Fogan, Moyang, and Tingeu. Then the Manchu Tartars invaded the region. Christians were targets of their hostility. In January 1648, in the city of Fogan, during the recitation of the Sorrowful Mysteries of the Most Holy Rosary, his enemies beheaded him.

In the early 18th century, during the age of the emperor Yung-Cheng, an edict of condemnation was proclaimed against five missionaries – Bishop Peter Sans and four priests, Francis Serrano, Joachim Royo, John Alcober, and Francis Diaz. They were sentenced to beheading "for having taught errors and having deceived the people with the same false doctrine." The decision of the emperor to judge Bishop Sans and his companions came on May 26, 1746. By this time, these holy men had already served their God well. It had been more than 40 years since the Bishop's ordination. Father Francis Serrano spent 20 years as a missionary and Father Royo exercised his apostolate for some 33 years. Father Alcober preached the Gospel for 20 years, while Father Diaz labored in the mission fields for 13 years. In the capital of Fukien, Bishop Sans spent 11 months in prison. Fathers Serrano and Royo were suffocated, while their confreres Alcober and Diaz were strangled in October 1748.

19th Century

The Catholic faith, which had been legalized by the Emperor Kang-Hi (1662-1723), was forbidden by his successors. The Emperor Kia-Kin (1796-1821) actively opposed the Catholic faith through the promulgation of frequent and severe decrees. In 1805, a decree outlawed the Catholic faith; another ordered "severe actions against all teachers of religion." In 1821, he declared "the religion of the Lord of Heaven must be rigorously prohibited" and ordered the punishment of "the priest-propagators of this religion as well as those stupid men who follow them." In 1840, under the reign of Toa-Kouany (1821-1850), a decree ordered apostates to trample upon a cross. Another decree, in 1842, made the same prescription and exiled those apostates who returned to the practice of the faith. By these edicts, many European and Chinese Christians were martyred throughout the provinces of China.

The Martyrs of the Society for the Foreign Missions of Paris (M.E.P.)

In 1775, immediately following his ordination, Gabriel Taurin Dufresse headed for the mission of Su-Tchuen in China where he was entrusted with the spiritual care of the northern part of the province. The Christians then were scattered among numerous villages and cites. In 1784, the Emperor Khien-long issued decrees of prohibition against the Europeans and their faith. Father Dufresse, with two other missionaries, was sent to prison in Bejiing. Six months later, he left for Macao, a convenient location to reach his mission territory of Tchen-Tou. He labored there for another decade. On December 15, 1801, he succeeded his bishop, who had died. The edicts of 1805 forced the bishop to continually flee prosecutors and live the life of a stray animal. However, in 1815, he was arrested, condemned and executed on Sept. 14, 1815.

Augustine Tchao was born in the province of Kouy-Tcheou to a pagan family. In 1785, as a soldier, he escorted Father Gabriel Dufresse to a Beijing prison. Being moved by Father Dufresse's enduring patience in the prison, he returned to the growing churches of the Su-Tchuen province, was baptized, and later became a diocesan priest.

From village to village, he brought to the faithful the consolation of the word of God and the sacraments. Toward the end of 1814, he was arrested, endured the cruelest torture, and suffered a most agonizing death in prison in 1815.

Like Father Tchao, Joseph Yuen, heard the saintly sermons of Bishop Dufresse, at which point the beauty of the Christian faith seized his heart. Later, Bishop Dufresse ordained him. Father Yuen evangelized in various places. Meanwhile, the persecutions under Emperor Kia-Kin grew worse. And he was arrested in August 1816. The tribunal employed flattery and threat in the hope of getting Father Yuen to betray the names and hiding places of the European and local priests. He languished in prison for nearly a year. He was strangled on June 24, 1817.

Following the martyrdom of Father Yuen, on August 15th, Father Paul Lieou, the youngest priest in Su-Tcheun, was arrested. Distinguished by his amiability, modesty and simplicity, the fury of the persecutions and injustices doubled his zeal. After his arrest, he was taken to Tchen-Tou, where the Mandarin examined him. Before the Mandarin he declared that he was a priest and ready to die rather than renounce the Catholic faith. He was beaten and locked up in prison, and strangled on Feb. 13, 1818.

In 1800, Joseph Tchang-Ta-Pong, was baptized at the age of 46. Previously a businessman, now he returned to Kouy-Yang, animated with missionary zeal. During this period the persecutions against the Christians intensified. Joseph was able to evade prosecution. However, he was betrayed for the price of "silver" by his brother in law, imprisoned and strangled on March 12, 1815.

Born of pagan families in the province of Kouy-Tcheou two lay catechists, Peter Lieou and Joachim Ho, converted to Catholicism in their early 20's. In the great persecution of 1814, they were arrested together and subjected to cruel torture. However, due to their steadfastness, they were condemned to exile to Tartaria along with other Christians. There they remained for nearly two decades. In 1834 Peter Lieou was arrested again and strangled on May 17th of that year. In 1839, Joachim Ho was arrested, refused to apostatize, and was strangled on July 9, 1839 by order of the Emperor.

After a long and difficult voyage, the 40-year old priest Father August Chapdelaine landed at Kouang-Si on December 3, 1854. From the moment he arrived, he was denounced and, finally, in 1856, taken before the Mandarin, he was told to renounce the Catholic faith. Refusing to do so, he was ferociously beaten and tortured, left to die in a cage, and then his decapitated corpse was fed to animals.

Two of Father Chapdelaine's catechists also met the same fate as he. Lawrence Pe-Man was a humble laborer, who was baptized at the age of 20 by Father Chapdelaine. From that moment, Lawrence became a fervent Christian and only death was able to separate him from his missionary zeal.

Threatened and tortured, nothing could make him apostatize. He was beheaded on Feb. 25, 1856. The other catechist, Agnes Tsao-Kouy was born to an old Christian family. After the death of her harsh and cruel husband, she worked with Father Chapdelaine. She instructed the newly-baptized young women of village and was greatly successful in this endeavor. In 1856, she was arrested and condemned to death in the cage.

The Martyrs of Mao-Keou

Mao-Keou is a district of the province of Kouy-Tcheou. From 1852, the Christian faith flourished there. Among the most meritorious of the Christian faithful are two catechists, Jerome Lou-Tin-Mei and Lawrence Ouang, and a virgin, Agatha Lin.

Jerome Lou-Tin-Mei brought Christianity to his entire family and converted 200 pagans to the Christian faith.

Lawrence Ouang, husband and father of five, was commissioned by the local Bishop to teach the faith which he performed with the greatest zeal wandering from village to village bringing pagans to the faith.

Agatha Lin, whose father was imprisoned for the faith consecrated herself to God from her youth. She dedicated herself to the task of teaching.

Because of their zeal and evangelization efforts, Jerome, Lawrence, and Agatha were brought before the local official who asked them to renounce their religion. After reaffirming their faith, they were beheaded in January 1858.

The Martyrs of Tsin-Gay

In June 1861, two seminarians of the Major Seminary of the province of Kouy-Tcheou, Joseph Tchang and Paul Tchen, a Christian layman, John-Baptist Lo, and a pious widow, Martha Ougan, were arrested. A convert to Catholicism, John Baptist Lo was a local farmer and served as the office administrator of the seminary. Martha Ougan was the seminary's cook. In the holy tradition of St. Martha's service to Our Lord, she made herself the servant of these three holy men during their imprisonment. These four followers of Christ suffered injustices for six weeks and were beheaded on July 29, 1861.

The Martyrs of Kay-Tcheou

In 1855, Jean-Peter Neel, entered the Seminary for the Foreign Missions of Paris. In 1859, he arrived in China and was soon founding and administering approximately 20 parishes. In 1862, the lives of four other martyrs of Kay-Tcheou, Martin Ou, John Tchang, John Tchen, and Lucy Y, were unified in their missionary zeal around the saintly leadership of this young priest.

Late in life, Martin Ou turned to the Lord and consecrated himself to the service of the mission, but only after fruitless attempts to save his wayward wife and failed marriage. As a catechist, he visited many villages, leaving everywhere traces and fruits of his travels.

John Tchang, a convert from Buddhism, expressed an admirable zeal for the renewal of the spirit through conversion. Only a few days after Father Neel baptized him with water, he joined Father Neel in the baptism of blood.

John Tchen, born into a pagan family, through conversations with Christians, he embraced the Catholic faith during mid-life and served the mission fields for over 25 years culminating his service at Father Neel's mission.

Lucy Y was baptized as an infant and as a young woman consecrated her virginity to God. She served as a catechist for over thirty years, serving her last year with Father Neel. On February 18, 1862, General Tien, a great enemy of the Christians, arrested Father Neel together with Martin Ou, John Tchang and John Tchen. They were taken outside the city and beheaded. Later that day, Lucy was imprisoned. She was beheaded the next day.

Francis Regis Clet of the Congregation of the Missions (C.M.)

Ordained a priest in 1773, Father Clet spent fifteen years as Professor of Theology at the Major Seminary of Annecy, France. Here he was held in such high esteem and so admired for his sanctity and great culture that he came to be known as the "living library". However in 1790, revolution struck and a mob broke into the Novitiate at San Lazar where he was the Director, bringing death and destruction. This cruel trial only prepared him for what was to come and he was forced to leave France. In April 1791, he left for the Orient.

For the next 30 years he lived the sacrificial life of a missionary, with an indefatigable zeal, he evangelized three immense provinces of the Chinese Empire. Since a violent persecution was underway, he was forced to leave his poor home and to flee into the woods and conceal himself among the caves; but one day he was betrayed by a Christian who knew where he was, and took the persecutors there to find him. Father Clet, just like Our Divine Lord, was sold to his persecutors for thirty silver pieces. Having been brought before the judges and thrown into prison, he appeared many times before the mandarins and the rulers of Ho-Nan: he was not spared any torture. No matter what was done to him, he never complained once. The Emperor in the end ordered him to be strangled on Feb. 17, 1820.

20th Century

In 1900, the missions in China suffered a grave threat from an uprising known as the Boxer Rebellion. Since the members of this group exercised gymnastics and boxing, their name was translated from the Chinese as the "Boxers." The Boxers targeted all: Catholics and Protestants, bishops, missionaries and lay Chinese Christians of every age and condition, man, woman and child. They destroyed what had been patiently and laboriously built by the Chinese missions over fifty years of peace. Throughout China, approximately 100,000 people were put to death for the Christian faith. In Shantung more than 200 missionary outposts were destroyed, more than 10,000 Christians scattered, of whom 200 shed their blood for the faith. Worse still was the violence that befell Shansi and Hunan where more than 30,000 Christians were murdered.

Martyrs of the OFM and Companions
Father John of Trier

In 1799, John of Trier, a priest of the OFM of the Roman province, reached Macao and proceeded to Hunan, his first field of missionary activity. There he remained for three years fervently preaching the Gospel. In 1804 he moved to Kiang-si, remaining there until 1812. In that province severe edicts were promulgated against Christianity and police informers were well compensated for turning in Christians.

In 1812, a catechist betrayed him to the mandarins as a European and a minister of the Christian religion. Soldiers attacked his home, but he escaped dressed as a peasant and took refuge in Hunan. In the summer of 1815, the persecution was exacerbated with the arrest and imprisonment of many missionaries and catechists, including Father John of Trier. Openly professing the faith of his baptism, he remained locked up in prison, until he was strangled on Feb. 7, 1816.

The Martyrs of Shansi

The martyrs at Shansi included nine Franciscan Friars, three of whom were bishops, seven Franciscan Missionaries of Mary, and five seminarians. The martyrs also included nine Chinese domestics, many of whom were third order Franciscans. While they could have defended themselves and fled, they preferred instead, to remain with their spiritual fathers and share the merit and glory of martyrdom on July 9, 1900.

In 1876, at the age of 43, Father Gregory Grassi, having already been on the mission fields for sixteen years, became coadjutor Bishop and Vicar Apostolic of Shansi. In 1891, he became responsible for the vicariate. He assiduously promoted confession, catechesis of children and adults, works of mercy for the poor and the needy, and supported and assisted the works of missionaries for several decades. On the vigil of his martyrdom, he was invited to flee and conceal himself, but he refused, saying, "I have desired and asked God to make me a martyr and now that I have reached this hoped for moment, why should I flee?"

Father Francis Fogolla left for the mission in China in 1866. He was destined to Tayuanfu, in Shansi, with Bishop Grassi. In his capacity as Vicar General, he dedicated himself to the spread of Christianity, the administration of the sacraments, to preach to Christians and non-Christians alike. At Paris they received the unexpected news that Father Fogolla was named coadjutor bishop of Bishop Grassi and he was consecrated back in Paris on August 14, 1898. He traveled through France, Belgium and England looking for help and support for the work of the missions.

Father Theodore Balat had many important duties: teaching in the minor seminary; novice master; promoter of the missions; and chaplain to the Franciscan Missionary Sisters of Mary. When the tyrant Ju-Sien came with his soldiers, he was peacefully reciting his breviary. He stood up, blessed the religious sisters and accompanied them courageously to torture, sharing with them the palm of martyrdom.

Bishop Fogolla was the one who brought the seven Franciscan Missionary Sisters of Mary to China on May 4, 1899. They arrived during the horror of the Boxer Rebellion in Shansi. The sisters were representative of Europe's missionary zeal since the group included three French women, two Italians, a Belgian, and a Dutchwoman. Though from different cultures, their common Catholic faith united them and they supported each other in their final step into eternal glory.

Mary Ermellina of Jesus (Irma Grivot) tempted to leave at the moment of the trial, protested forcefully that she was there to give her blood for Jesus Christ.

Mary of Peace (Mary Ann Giuliani), an enthusiastically musical soul approached death's door leading the sisters in the triumphant hymn, Te Deum.

Mary Clare (Clelia Nanetti) lived a life of meditation, work, and intense piety. This thoroughly prepared her for martyrdom and she led the sisters to the place of torture and was the first beheaded.

Mary of St. Natalie (Joan Mary Kerguin), characterized by her untiring work, was filled in a supernatural atmosphere of Franciscan joy, even when surrounded by the physical suffering.

Mary of St. Justin (Anna Moreau) was a true model of activity and piety.

Maria Adolphina (Anna Dierk) was a model of total servitude and obedience doing work from morning to night and often spending the silent hours of the night serving all.

The Chinese called Mary Amandina (Paula Jeuris) "the European virgin who always smiles." Coming to China, they served in the mission fields for just over one year together, but now reign in eternal bliss together.

Elia Facchini was ordained on Dec. 18, 1964. In 1866 he asked and received an assignment to the missions in Tayuanfu. Father Facchini served as rector of the local seminary, where he taught Letters and Theology. At the beginning of 1900, he said of his coming martyrdom, "My body is already worn out. I thank the Lord if I must die for the faith." These were his last words.

A group of five pious and virtuous seminarians, some still in their teens, were examples of strength and serenity beyond their years and they met their death together. They included John Tchang, Patrick Tun, John Van, Philip Tchang, and John Tchang.

Bishop Grassi entrusted Father Andrew Bauer with the direction of lay personnel of his household and the hospital. Throughout the storm of 1900, he anticipated martyrdom, as indicated when he wrote his brother saying, "We are at the dawn of a new century - I do not know what awaits us: oh, if I was able to steal - like the good thief - I would be in Paradise." Several months later, a soldier asked him for his hands to bind them, Andrew prostrated himself before him, kissed the chain, and singing was lead off to the torture chamber.

The third order Franciscans worked ardently as domestics but also fervently as models of fidelity and obedience. They worked in the fields, served the missions and orphanages, and took care of the Episcopal residences. They manifested a deep and holy passion intertwining their work with devotions, such as praying the Most Holy Rosary.

The tertiaries that died alongside their Bishops Grassi and Fogolla included Thomas Sen-Ki-Kuo, Simon Tceng, Peter U-Ngan-Pan, Francis Tchang-Iun, Matthew Fun-Te, and Peter Tciang. There were three members of the humble class of poorest peasants who confessed their faith, rather than fleeing to the hills for safety, and, thus, sealed their death warrant. James Ien-ku-Tun prepared vegetables for the table of the missionaries; James Tciao-Tciuen-Sin led a poor, servile and virtuous life; and Peter Wang-Ol-Man grew up in the mission's orphanage and was a servant in the seminary's kitchen.

The Martyrs of Southern Hunan
The Boxer Rebellion spread to Hunan on July 4, 1900, with acts of brutality and rallying cries of "death to the Europeans." There was whole scale sacking, arson and destruction of churches and residences. Old Christian families were attacked, while the Mandarin Decrees were promulgated against the faith.

It was only one year after Father Cesidio Giacomantonino began his apostolate in China that he was surrounded by the chaos of the Boxer Rebellion mob. In order to protect the Blessed Sacrament, he quickly went to the chapel to consume the Sacrament. He was mortally wounded by a blow from a spear. He was wrapped in a covering, doused in oil and set on fire. He died, on July 4, 1900, not yet 27-years-old.

In 1867, Antonino Fantosati, with a small group of companions, among whom was Father Elia Facchini, left for China. After more than 20 years of assiduous and fruitful work, he was chosen to be Vicar Apostolic of South Hunan.

Father Joseph Mary Gambaro reached China in March 1896. He was entrusted with the responsibility of teaching the local aspirants for the seminary in intellectual and spiritual endeavors. He then went to spread the Christian faith in Yen-tciou, where it was accepted enthusiastically by all.

Bishop Fantosati realized the coming violence of the Boxer Rebellion and prepared himself with courage. On July 7, 1900, he was returning by boat from a pastoral visit accompanied by Fr. Joseph Gambaro, and other Christians. Bishop Fantosati's ship was attacked. Father Gambaro suffered a horrible death from numerous blows to the body. As he was dying, the Bishop raised his hands to bless him. From the bank, the Bishop attempted to calm the crowd, but a blow to the head brought him crashing to the ground, where he lay in agony for two hours before his death.

The Martyrs of the Society of Jesus and Companions

This group of martyrs, four French Jesuit missionary priests and 52 lay Chinese Christians, evidence the deep ecclesial bond between the preachers of the Gospel and the fervent Chinese faithful.

Modesto Andlauer was ordained in 1876 and sent to China in 1882 accompanied by Remigio Isore. Leo Mangin, born in France and educated in Belgium, left for China in 1882. For four years he studied Chinese and theology along with Remigio Isore, who were both ordained in 1886. After many years of caring for his widowed mother, Paul Denn came to China and was ordained in 1880.

Father Andlauer was a man of intense prayer, while Father Isore was an austere religious and a very energetic missionary. In June 1900, while on retreat, Father Isore heard about the Boxer incursions into his parish. Returning to be with his people in this hour of darkness, along the way he stopped at Ou-Y, Father Andlauer's mission. On June 19, 1900, hearing the crackling of the gunfire of the Boxers very close, the two Jesuits repaired to the church and knelt there in prayer. The Boxers entered the sanctuary and pierced the missionaries with spears. Their blood splattered on the altar, and the men died as sacrificed lambs in imitation of the "Lamb of God."

Father Mangin was destined for the mission at Tchou-kia-ho. This village normally consisted of only 400, but on account of the attacks of the Boxers, refugees swelled the population nearer to 3,000. Foreseeing an attack of the Boxers, Fr. Mangin with the help of Father Denn attempted to fortify the village at Tchou-kia-ho. The Boxers made their first assault on the village on July 15, 1900, but the inhabitants put up a fierce resistance. However, on July 18, the Boxers penetrated the barricades and entered the village. Gathering the women and children in the church, Fathers Mangin and Denn, stood at the altar and led the soon-to-be martyrs in prayer. The Boxers broke down the doors of the church. As an outward manifestation of their professed faith the two priests were dressed in ecclesial vestments, and thus, they were among the first to die.

During the summer months of 1900, in southeastern Tcheli, the apostolic vicariate of Sien-Hsien, entrusted to the Jesuits, more than 5,000 members of the faithful were murdered in churches, along roadsides, in streets of towns and villages. They accompanied and shared in their French priests ultimate sacrifice. Of those that died, fifty-two Chinese Catholic faithful men, women and children, ages from 9 to 79, are numbered among the Blessed Chinese Martyrs.

Albert Crescitelli of the Pontifical Institute for the Foreign Missions (P.I.M.E.)

Albert Crescitelli was ordained on July 4, 1887, and left for the missions in south Shansi, China, the following year. He was martyred during the Boxer Rebellion on July 21, 1900.

Martyrs of the Salesian Society of St. John Bosco

In February 1930, Bishop Louis Versiglia, Vicar Apostolic of Shiu-chow and Father Callistus Caravario, pastor of Lin-chow, were traveling by boat with numerous companions. The two missionaries were murdered while they tried to safeguard the honor of the young women in their traveling group.

Christine Haapala taught CCD for many years and through that experience the ideas for writing works based on Scriptures and the Most Holy Rosary emerged. Her first book From Genesis to Revelation: Seven Scriptural Rosaries, *published in 1996 by Christendom Press, has been called "the encyclopedia of Scriptural Rosaries." Collaborating with Saint Gabriel Media, Christine Haapala wrote and recorded a Scriptural Rosary* The Sanctity of Life Scriptural Rosary *that awakens all to God's message of the dignity and sanctity of life. Her two most recent works,* The Suffering Servant's Courage *and* Speak, Lord, I am Listening *(a children's book) are published by Suffering Servant Scriptorium, a company she founded in the Jubilee Year.*

Father Matthew Carr is a parochial vicar at Holy Spirit Catholic Church in Annandale, Virginia. He attended seminary at the Pontifical North American College and pre-theology at St. Charles Borromeo Seminary in Philadelphia, Pennsylvania. Prior to seminary he earned a Master's Degree in Politics from the Catholic University of America and a Bachelors of Arts in History from the State University of New York at Binghamton.

Tim Drake

The Divine Mercy Saint:
Saint Faustina Kowalska

By Mark Kwasny

"Of course you are a saint. Soon I Myself will make this manifest in you, and they will pronounce the same word, saint, only this time it will be with love." [1650] So wrote Sister Faustina Kowalska in her celebrated diary, *Divine Mercy in My Soul*. As the first of the blesseds to be canonized in the Great Jubilee Year 2000, it should have come as no surprise to her or to anyone else that her sainthood would be inevitable.

It was April 30, 2000, on a brilliant sunny spring day in Rome that Blessed Faustina became Saint Faustina. Before a crowd of 200,000 jubilant pilgrims and onlookers, Pope John Paul II proclaimed, "Today my joy is truly great in presenting the life and witness of Sister Faustina Kowalska to the whole Church as a gift of God for our time... It is important then that we accept the whole message that comes to us from the word of God on this Second Sunday of Easter, which from now on throughout the Church will be called 'Divine Mercy Sunday'". After the many uncertainties that Saint Faustina experienced about the work of the Divine Mercy, the work came to fruition just as it was shown to her in a vision on March 23, 1937:

> I saw the Lord Jesus in our chapel, exposed in the monstrance on the high altar. The chapel was adorned as for a feast, and on that day anyone who wanted to come was allowed in. The crowd was so enormous that the eye could not take it all in. Everyone was participating in the celebrations with great joy, and many of them obtained what they desired. The same celebration was held in Rome, in a beautiful church, and the Holy Father, with all the clergy, was celebrating this Feast ... [1044]

God used a simple peasant girl, lowly and humble, to perform a great work for the Church and the world. In our world today, where so many people exult the rich, the famous, and the popular, this seemingly insignificant individual, born Helena Kowalska, was to become a servant of God bearing a message of mercy that the world needed so badly in her time and in the world today.

Saint Mary Faustina Kowalska was born Helena Kowalska on August 25, 1905 in a little village called Glogowiec in what was then a part of

Poland. Helena was one of ten children (although two died in infancy) born to Stanislaus and Marianna Kowalski. Interestingly, Marianna's first two births were complicated and difficult. But Helena was born into the world with no complications. Her brothers and sisters that followed were born likewise. Even at birth, Helena was bringing relief and joy to suffering souls.

Helena's parents were devout Catholics who made their faith a part of their everyday family life. Helena's father made it part of his daily ritual to sing the Little Hours of the Immaculate Conception [1 p.15, bio]. He also never missed Sunday Mass. Helena too was devoted to God at an early age and was zealous for the faith. She would work to finish her chores on Sundays so that she could attend Mass and would make up stories based on the lives of the saints to tell to neighboring children who followed her around. Already at age 7, Helena received an inspiration from God to lead a holy and sanctified life. And even earlier, she was known to wake in the middle of the night praying as she felt she was being led by her guardian angel. All of these experiences certainly pointed to the fact that God had special plans for Helena, but as she later stated, "...I did not always obey the call of grace. I did not know anyone who might have explained these things to me." [2 p.17, bio].

In 1917, at the age of 12, Helena started attending school, starting in the second grade because she already knew how to read. Because of World War I and the occupation of Poland by Russia, the schools had been closed prior to this time. In 1919, she was forced to leave school when it was decided that the older children must leave to make room for the younger ones. This was to be the only formal schooling Helena received in her life. This makes even more impressive the fact that the *Diary* she later authored at the command of the Lord Jesus Christ was over 600 pages in length.

At the age of 15, Helena decided that she wanted to get a job to bring in money to help pay for clothing and other necessities for her family. She worked as a maid but left after working for less than a year. She felt a stronger yearning for God and knew she was being gently guided toward work in His service. When she expressed her desire to leave home to enter a convent, her parents refused citing their inability to pay the necessary dowry that was needed to pay for her religious clothing and expenses.

Disappointed but undaunted, Helena left home in 1922 to look for work. After taking and leaving one job, she ended up working as a babysitter and maid in 1923. Before this, she decided to ask her parents again if she could leave to join a convent and once again, their answer was negative. Saddened by their response, Helena put more emphasis on worldly pleasures such as dancing and fashionable dress as she thought that her parents' refusal had put an end to her desire to enter the religious life. Even though she tried to put off the promptings of the Spirit, Helena found no satisfaction in these worldly things. The conflict in her soul continued until a decisive event turned things around.

According to her *Diary*, Helena was at a dance in Lodz with one of her sisters. The young people were dancing and enjoying themselves while her soul was experiencing what she termed as "deep torments." Suddenly, Jesus Himself appeared to her, "racked with pain, stripped of His clothing, all covered with wounds, who spoke these words to me: How long shall I put up with you and how long will you keep putting me off?" [9, p.7] After feigning a headache to her sister and friends, she left the dance and hastened to the Cathedral of Saint Stanislaus Kostka. It was there that Helena heard the words from Our Lord, "Go at once to Warsaw; you will enter a convent there." [10, p.7]

So at the age of eighteen, Helena Kowalska found herself on a journey to find a convent in a city where she knew no one. Trust was the message that the Lord would deliver to her and trust was the thing she needed most. Helena's life long journey was one marked by faith and trust in things she knew little about. But her love was for God and it was this desire to love and serve Him that pushed her further. Here was a young woman who had no spiritual director or confessor, only two years of formal education, and no guide other than the trust she placed in the interior inspirations she was receiving. Yet humility and obedience to the will of God would be her trademark for the years to come.

Frightened and uncertain where to go, the Lord directed her to the pastor of St. James Church in Warsaw where she divulged everything. The pastor, Fr. James Dabrowski, sent her to Mrs. Aldona Lipszycowa where she would stay until she found a convent that would accept her. After being sent away from several convents that she called upon, Helena knocked on the door of the Congregation of the Sister of Our Lady of Mercy in Warsaw.

The Mother Superior of the convent came to the door and after a short conversation, told Helena that if the Lord of the house accepted her, then she would too. Helena went to the chapel and asked the Lord if He would accept her and at once she heard, "I do accept; you are in My Heart." And so it was here that young Helena Kowalska would begin her incredible journey that the Lord would lead her upon.

On April 30, 1926, Helen received her veil and would now be known as Sister Mary Faustina. Sr. Faustina was full of zeal and happiness, yet even still, she was soon plunged into what is known as the Dark Night of the soul. Toward the end of the first year of her novitiate, she began to experience the misery of her own soul and she was unable to find comfort in her prayers and supplications to the Lord or to any of the saints. She got to the point of feeling that God had rejected her and that somehow she was the object of

His just anger. Her soul was full of despair and she had to fight the darkness that was overwhelming her soul. After months of being in this state, she was visited one night by the Mother of God [25] who visited her holding the Infant Jesus in Her arms. Sr. Faustina said, "Mary, my Mother, do You know how terribly I suffer?" at which Mary replied, "*I know how much you suffer, but do not be afraid. I share with you your suffering, and I shall always do so.*" But even this heavenly vision only brought her joy and consolation for a day as Sr. Faustina found her soul once again plunged into spiritual torment. But she was so intent on doing the will of God and pleasing Him that she prayed with humility and sincerity, "Forgive me, Jesus; may Your holy will be done in me. I will suffer silently like a dove, without complaining. I will not allow my heart even one single cry of sorrowful complaint."

In reading her *Diary*, it is already obvious at a very early stage that Sr. Faustina is working toward total abandonment of her soul to God. Hers was not a life without suffering or difficulties, but her desire to serve God was above all else and allowed her to accept everything that God sent to her, the joys and the pains. What was so extraordinary about Sr. Faustina's life was not that she did anything grandiose for everyone to see, rather, she used each moment of her life to be an example of Christ to others in every circumstance.

During her novitiate, a confessor gave her instruction that Sr. Faustina obviously took to heart:

> Act in such a way that all those who come in contact with you will go away joyful. Sow happiness about you because you have received much from God; give, then, generously to others. They should take leave of you with their hearts filled with joy, even if they have no more than touched the hem of your garment. Keep well in mind the words I am telling you right now. [55, p. 28]

Opportunities to practice this advice were all around her, but one notable example took place on September 6, 1937. Sr. Faustina was given the assignment of gatekeeper for the convent where she was to answer any visitors who came to the gate. While this would be a great opportunity to practice mercy, it also caused her some unease as she had heard that it could be a dangerous task due to the fact that there were "revolutionary disturbances" at the time and that there were many people who had a hatred for convents and religious. [1271, p.459] But Jesus gave her to know that He was helping her and she in fact had several occasions to assist others while in this position, especially the poor and destitute. It was a shining example of Jesus' words, "As you did it to one of the least of these my brethren, you did it to me." [Matt. 25:40] that Sr. Faustina relates in her *Diary* that shows so vividly how Jesus wants us to practice mercy in our lives. It was during her duties as gatekeeper that Sr. Faustina records the instance when a poor young man came to the convent gate:

> This young man, emaciated, barefoot and bareheaded, and with his clothes in tatters, was frozen because the day was cold and rainy. He asked for something hot to eat. So I went to the kitchen, but found nothing there for the poor. But, after searching around for some time, I succeeded in finding some soup, which I reheated and into which I crumbled some bread, and I gave it to the poor young man, who ate it. As I was taking the bowl from him, he gave me to know that He was the Lord of heaven and earth. When I saw Him as He was, He vanished from my sight. When I went back in and reflected on what had happened at the gate, I heard these words in my soul: My daughter, the blessing of the poor who bless Me as they leave this gate have reached My ears. And your compassion, within the bounds of obedience, has pleased Me, and this is why I came down from My throne — to taste the fruits of your mercy. [1312, p.472]

Jesus had asked that Sr. Faustina be the secretary and messenger of The Divine Mercy to the world, and her journey toward Heaven was marked with mercy.

It was on February 22, 1931, that Jesus first revealed to Sr. Faustina the image of The Divine Mercy that would later become an icon of devotion around the world. What Sr. Faustina was given to know was the depths of God's mercy and His desire that all mankind be drawn to the abyss of His mercy through this image:

> In the evening, when I was in my cell, I saw the Lord Jesus clothed in a white garment. One hand [was] raised in the gesture of blessing, the other was touching the garment at the breast. From beneath the garment, slightly drawn aside at the breast, there were emanating two large rays, one red, the other pale. In silence I kept my gaze fixed on the Lord; my soul was struck with awe, but also with great joy. After a while, Jesus said to me, Paint an image according to the pattern you see, with the signature: Jesus, I trust in You.

> I desire that this image be venerated, first in your chapel, and [then] throughout the world. I promise that the soul that will venerate this image will not perish. I also promise victory over [its] enemies already here on earth, especially at the hour of death. I Myself will defend it as My own glory.

And later, the Lord told her:

> I desire that there be a Feast of Mercy. I want this image, which you will paint with a brush, to be solemnly blessed on the first Sunday after Easter; that Sunday is to be the Feast of Mercy. [47-49, p.24]

This message of mercy is summed up by Fr. George Kosicki, CSB, administrator for the Divine Mercy International (DMI) apostolate at the Marian Helpers Center in Stockbridge, Massachusetts:

> The *message* of Divine Mercy is that God is merciful. He is love itself poured out for us, and He wants no one to escape that merciful love. The message is that God wants us to turn to Him with trust and repentance while it is still a time of mercy — before He comes as the Just Judge — a time of mercy that is a preparation for His Second Coming. This turning with trust to Him who is mercy itself is the only source of peace for mankind, the only answer to the troubled world — there is no escaping that answer. [p.1, Now is the Time for Mercy]

Along with the image of the Divine Mercy, Jesus entreated Sr. Faustina to recite the prayers that went along with it. He revealed these to her while she was praying in the convent chapel. The prayers are said on the beads of an ordinary Rosary with the following prayers:

First of all, you will say one *Our Father* and *Hail Mary* and the *I Believe in God*. Then on the *Our Father* beads you will say the following words: "Eternal Father, I offer You the Body and Blood, Soul and Divinity of your dearly beloved Son, Our Lord Jesus Christ, in atonement for our sins and those of the whole world." On the *Hail Mary* beads you will say the following words: "For the sake of His sorrowful Passion have mercy on us and on the whole world." In conclusion, three times you will recite these words: "Holy God, Holy Mighty One, Holy Immortal One, have mercy on us and on the whole world."

And so with the revelation of the image and prayers to The Divine Mercy, Sr. Faustina embarked on her mission to let the world know of God's mercy and worked to bring it about in her. Yet even with revelations from the Lord, Sr. Faustina harbored doubts and confusion as to what the Lord was asking Her to do while at the same time unsure as to how she could carry out His will for her and the world.

It was during one of these periods of uncertainty that Sr. Faustina went to confession to reveal what was on her soul. She thought that her visits from the Lord were illusions and she was hoping to get some direction or at least affirmation that it was indeed the Lord Jesus who was leading her. After Sr. Faustina had spoken about her concerns, the confessor told her: "I cannot discern what power is at work in you, Sister; perhaps it is God and perhaps it is the evil spirit." [211, p.109] In her *Diary*, she recounts how her confusion made her want to stop listening to the Lord's voice in these revelations altogether. "There was one thing I could not understand for a long time: Jesus ordered me to tell everything to my Superiors, but my Superiors did not believe what I said and treated me with pity as though I were being deluded or were imagining things. Because of this, believing myself to be deluded, I resolved to avoid God interiorly for fear of these illusions." [38, p.20]

What gave Sr. Faustina much concern too was that she had no regular confessor to which she could bare her soul and receive guidance. She prayed hard that the Lord would provide her with one and in return, Jesus granted two visions to her of her earthly help and guide. Sr. Faustina saw in a vision the Reverend Professor Michael Sopocko. In the vision, she saw him standing between the altar and the confessional when she heard an interior voice say: This is the visible help for you on earth. He will help you carry out My will on earth. And so Sr. Faustina had the help for which she had yearned and prayed so hard. Fr. Sopocko was not only to be her confessor and spiritual guide, but he was also to be responsible for helping establish all that the Lord was commanding Sr. Faustina concerning The Divine Mercy as well as the suffering that would go along with it.

So Sr. Faustina went ahead in obedience to her superiors and her confessor in carrying out the Divine Will of Jesus in bringing about the Feast of Mercy. But Jesus was quite adamant that she — like all Christians then and now — must first practice mercy and be totally confident and trusting in the Divine Mercy of Jesus.

> My daughter, if I demand through you that people revere My mercy, you should be the first to distinguish yourself by this confidence in My mercy. I demand from you deeds of mercy, which are to arise out of love for Me.

You are to show mercy to your neighbors always and everywhere. You must not shrink from this or try to excuse or absolve yourself from it...Yes, the first Sunday after Easter is the Feast of Mercy, but there must also be acts of mercy, and I demand the worship of My mercy through the solemn celebration of the Feast and through the veneration of the image which is painted. By means of this image I shall grant many graces to souls. It is to be a reminder of the demands of My mercy, because even the strongest faith is of no avail without works.

The image of The Divine Mercy was first exposed to the public on April 26-28, 1935 [Life of Faustina Kowalska, p.96] at Ostra Brama. At first, Fr. Sopocko did not believe that the event would take place. The odds of the unknown painting of The Divine Mercy being hung in a church and then being preached about seemed insurmountable. Yet Sr. Faustina had told Fr. Sopocko that this is what the Lord had requested, and sure enough, the pieces fell into place. The pastor of the church, Reverend Canon Stanislaus Zawadzki, asked Fr. Sopocko to give the sermon for the Mass. Fr. Sopocko asked that the painting be hung near an icon of Our Lady which at first was denied. But the local archbishop gave permission for the painting to be hung and everything was in order for the exposition of the image.

Sr. Faustina was asked to help adorn the painting in the church and she gladly agreed to it. As she recounts in the *Diary*, the display of the image was momentous indeed:

When the image was displayed, I saw a sudden movement of the hand of Jesus, as He made a large sign of the cross. In the evening of the same day, when I had gone to bed, I saw the image going over the town, and the town was covered with what appeared to be a mesh and nets. As Jesus passed, He cut through all the nets and finally made a large sign of the cross and disappeared.

Jesus then told her, "You are a witness of My mercy. You shall stand before My throne forever as a living witness to My mercy."

This work of The Divine Mercy that Sr. Faustina was cooperating with the Lord to present to the world was already having its intended effects. After the sermon from Fr. Sopocko, she headed out of the church to get back home:

"When I had taken a few steps, a great multitude of demons blocked my way. They threatened me with terrible tortures, and voices could be heard:

"She has snatched away everything we have worked for over so many years!" When I asked them, "Where have you come from in such great numbers?" the wicked forms answered, "Out of human hearts; stop tormenting us!"

The task of executing God's will in bringing about the devotion and Feast of Divine Mercy would have been a difficult task for anyone to have taken on, but for Sr. Faustina, it was complicated by the fact that she had been diagnosed as having tuberculosis. She was to spend a great deal of time in hospitals and sanatoriums receiving treatment to help her through her pain. But as Sr. Faustina saw it, it was yet another way to suffer for souls and keep them from the clutches of Hell.

By August of 1937, the work concerning The Divine Mercy was progressing even though some difficulties still existed. In November, the litany, chaplet, and novena to The Divine Mercy were published in a pamphlet entitled, *Christ, King of Mercy*. The cover of the pamphlet depicted the picture of the Merciful Christ and the signature, "Jesus, I Trust in You." [Now is the time…p. 86] But with all the progress being made, it was clear to Sr. Faustina that this work would come under severe trial. And not only would the work suffer, so would Fr. Sopocko:

> There will come a time when this work, which God is demanding so very much, will be as though utterly undone. And then God will act with great power, which will give evidence of its authenticity…When this triumph comes, we shall already have entered the new life in which there is no suffering. But before this, your soul [of the spiritual director] will be surfeited with bitterness at the sight of the destruction of your efforts. However, this will only appear to be so, because what God has once decided upon, He does not change. But although this destruction will be such only in outward appearance, the suffering will be real. [378, p. 171]

She later records that:

> The glory of the Divine Mercy is resounding, even now, in spite of the efforts of its enemies and of Satan himself, who has a great hatred for God's mercy. This work will snatch a great number of souls from him, and that is why the spirit of darkness sometimes tempts good people violently, so that they may hinder the work. But I have clearly seen that the will of God is already being carried out,

and that it will be accomplished to the very last detail. The enemy's greatest efforts will not thwart the smallest detail of what the Lord has decreed. No matter if there are times when the work seems to be completely destroyed; it is then that the work is being all the more consolidated. [1659, .589]

On November 10, 1937, Sr. Faustina's superior, Mother Irene, brought the booklet containing the chaplet, the litany to the Divine Mercy, and the novena prayers to Sr. Faustina. As she was looking it over, the Lord spoke to her interiorly saying, "Already there are many souls who have been drawn to My love by this image. My mercy acts in souls through this work." So with God's help, the work of The Divine Mercy was spreading and souls were being saved. Sr. Faustina continued to work with Fr. Sopocko to further the work. But even as her zeal for saving souls increased, her health continued to deteriorate.

In April of 1938, Sr. Faustina was sent to a sanatorium in Pradnik for what would turn out to be her final stay. She continued to offer her sufferings for souls and on several occasions, prayed earnestly for those who had either died or were on their deathbeds. It was made known to her by Jesus that her prayers kept these souls from going to Hell. In one of the last entries in the *Diary*, she writes that, "Many souls are receiving graces [from the image], although they do not speak of it openly. Even though it has met up with all sorts of vicissitudes, God is receiving glory because of it; and the efforts of Satan and of evil men are shattered and come to naught. In spite of Satan's anger, The Divine Mercy will triumph over the whole world and will be worshiped by all souls." [1789, p.632]

Sr. Faustina was taken back home to Crakow on September 17 where she awaited her death. On September 26, Fr. Sopocko visited Sr. Faustina for the last time and later wrote, "She looked like an unearthly being." It was a couple of weeks later on October 5 that Sr. Faustina made her final Confession and then died after succumbing to the advanced stages of tuberculosis.

The passing of Sr. Faustina from this world did not mean an end to the spreading of the devotion. World War II broke out shortly after her death and The Divine Mercy was a source of strength during those difficult times. The devotion made its way to America in 1941 and proliferated to the point where millions of copies of the prayer cards were printed and disseminated throughout the world. It seemed as though word of The Divine Mercy would find its way into every nook and cranny of the globe, but the earlier prophecy that Sr. Faustina had made about this work was soon to come to pass.

The prophecy concerning the seeming destruction of the devotion was fulfilled when on November 28, 1958, the Holy See, acting upon inaccurate and insufficient information concerning the revelations, issued a decree of condemnation banning the devotion to The Divine Mercy.

Part of the explanation to the Polish Church hierarchy was that "the revelations of Sister Faustina Kowalska do not bear the characteristics of supernatural origin." [Now is the Time...p. 95] On March 6, 1959, Pope John XXIII replaced the ban with a "Notification" prohibiting "the spreading of images and writings that propose the devotion of The Divine Mercy *in the forms proposed by the same Sister Faustina*." As a result, many priests stopped preaching about The Divine Mercy and it seemed as though dead. But the Notification had allowed local bishops the discretion to decide what was to be done with the images already in place in the churches. As a result, the images and everything having to do with the devotion were withdrawn. In Crakow where the Sisters of Our lady of Mercy resided, the Archbishop allowed the image to remain in the side altar and also instructed that the faithful not be hindered from praying before the image for graces. This happens to be where the body of Sr. Faustina was buried at the time.

It wasn't until 1963, when the Prefect of Office of the Holy See, Cardinal Ottaviani, gave instructions to the archbishop actively promoting the beatification of Sr. Faustina to hurry and interview the witnesses before they all died. The archbishop had been elevated to the office of Cardinal and finished the Process of Information on September 20, 1967. The Process of Information was received in Rome on January 26, 1968 and by a decree of the Sacred Congregation for the Causes of Saints on January 31, 1968, beatification of the Servant of God, Sister Faustina Kowalska, was formally inaugurated.

On April 15, 1978, the Holy See reversed its Notification of 1958 and again allowed the spreading of the devotion to The Divine Mercy. The man primarily responsible for this achievement was Karol Cardinal Wojtyla, the Archbishop of Crakow who six months later was elevated to the See of Peter as Pope John Paul II.

On April 18, 1993, Sr. Faustina was beatified in Rome on the Second Sunday of Easter, after the healing of Maureen Digan at the tomb of Sr. Faustina was verified as having been a miracle. And on that glorious sun-drenched day in Rome on April 30, 2000, Pope John Paul II presided over the canonization of Sr. Faustina. As if to satisfy the command of the Lord, the Holy Father made the Sunday after Easter a universal feast to The Divine Mercy. As the joyful crowd gave its enthusiastic approval, the Pope offered hope to an aching world in his praises of Sr. Faustina and The Divine Mercy:

And you, Faustina, a gift of God to our time, a gift from the land of Poland to the whole Church, obtain for us an awareness of the depth of divine mercy; help us to have a living experience of it and to bear witness to it among our brothers and sisters. May your message of light and hope spread throughout the world, spurring sinners to conversion, calming rivalries, hatred, opening individuals, and nations to the practice of brotherhood. Today, fixing our gaze with you on the face of the risen Christ, let us make our own your prayer of trusting abandonment and say with firm hope: Christ Jesus, I trust in you! Jezu, ufam tobie!

Mark Kwasny is the founder of the Catholic Writer's Association and a free-lance writer. He lives in Ashburn, Virginia with his wife and four children.

Appendix

Tim Drake

Appendix A
List of Those Beatified/Canonized During the Jubilee Year 2000

March 5, 2000
Beatifications
André de Soveral

Ambrósio Francisco Ferro and 28 Companions

Andrew of Phú Yén

Maria Stella Mardosewicz and 10 Companions

Nicolas Bunkerd Kitbamrung

Pedro Calungsod

April 9, 2000
Beatifications

Mariano de Jesus Euse Hoyos

Francis Xavier Seelos

Anna Rosa Gattorno

Maria Elisabetta Hesselblad

Mariam Theresia Chiramel Mankidiyan

April 30, 2000
Canonization

Beata Maria Faustina (Elena Kowalska)

May 13, 2000
Beatifications
Jacinta and Francisco Marto of Fatima

May 21, 2000
Beatifications
Cristoforo Magallanes and 24 Companions

Giuseppe Maria de Yermo Y Parres

Maria di Gesu Sacramentato (Maria Venegas de la Torre)

September 3, 2000
Beatifications
Pope Pio IX (Giovannie Maria Mastai Ferretti)

Pope John XXIII (Angelo Giuseppe Roncalli)

Tommaso Reggio

Guillaume-Joseph Chaminade

Columba Marmion

October 1, 2000
Canonizations
Agostino Tchao, Pietro Tchou, Anna Wang, Francesco Fernandez de Capillas, Gabriele Taurin Dufresse, Gregorio Grassi, Leone Ignazio Mangin, and 113 Companions.

Maria Giuseppa del Cuore di Gesu' Sancho de Guerra

Katharine Maria Drexel

Josephine Bakhita

Appendix B
Litany of the Blessed Chinese Martyrs
By Christine Haapala

LORD, have mercy.
Christ, have mercy.
Lord, have mercy.

God the Father, Almighty and Merciful God, have mercy on us.
God the Son, Lamb of God, have mercy on us.
God the Holy Spirit, Breath of Life, have mercy on us.
Jesus, Our Refuge, have mercy on us.
Jesus, Strength of Martyrs, have mercy on us.
Heart of Jesus, Pierced with a lance, have mercy on us.
Heart of Jesus, Hope of those who die in you, have mercy on us.
Blood of Christ, Poured out at the cross, have mercy on us.
Blood of Christ, Courage of Martyrs, have mercy on us.

Immaculate Mary, Mother of the Crucified Christ, pray for us.
Immaculate Mary, Comfort of the Afflicted, pray for us.
Immaculate Mary, Queen of Martyrs, pray for us.

Blessed Chinese Martyrs, harshly treated, pray for us.
Blessed Chinese Martyrs, beaten down on every side, pray for us.
Blessed Chinese Martyrs, afflicted day after day and chastised in the
    morning,

Blessed Chinese Martyrs, beaten and in pain,
Blessed Chinese Martyrs, insulted, persecuted and slandered,
Blessed Chinese Martyrs, delivered over to the sword,
Blessed Chinese Martyrs, slaughtered at the evening twilight,
Blessed Chinese Martyrs, mortally afflicted,
Blessed Chinese Martyrs, hearts poured out to God,
Blessed Chinese Martyrs, standing at the victory gate,
Blessed Chinese Martyrs, at rest in God alone,
Blessed Chinese Martyrs, sheltered in the shadow of His wings,
Blessed Chinese Martyrs, crowned in glory,

St. Augustine Tchao, pray for us,
St. John Alcober Figuera,
St. Modesto Andlauer,

St. Theodore Balat,
St. Andrew Bauer,
St. Callistus Caravario,
St. Joseph Chang,
St. Joseph Chang-Ta-Pong,
St. Augustine Chapdelaine,
St. Paul Chen,
St. Mary Clare,
St. Albert Crescitelli,
St. Paul Denn,
St. Francis Díaz del Rincón,
St. Elia Facchini,
St. Mary Fan-K'Ounn,
St. Anthony Fantosati,
St. Francis Fernández de Capillas
St. Francis Fogolla,
St. Mary Fou,
St. Matthew Fun-Te,
St. Cesidio Giacomantonio,
St. Gregory Grassi,
St. Mary Hermina of Jesus,
St. Joachim Ho,
St. James Ien-Ku-Tun,
St. Remigio Isoré,
St. Paul Keue-T'Ing-Tchou,
St. Theresa Kinn-Tsie,
St. K'I-Tchou-Tzeu,
St. Mark Ki-T'Ien-Siang,
St. Mary Kouo-Li-Cheu,
St. Paul Lang-Eull,
St. Lang-Yang-Cheu,
St. Paul Lieou,
St. Peter Lieou,
St. Thaddeus Lieou,
St. Agatha Lin,
St. Paul Liou-Tsinn-Tei,
St. Peter Liou-Tzeu-U,
St. Peter Li-Ts'Uan,
St. Raymond Li-Ts'Uan,
St. John-Baptist Lô,
St. Leo Ignatius Mangin,
St. Jerome Lou-Tin-Mei,

St. Joseph Mary Gambaro
St. Joseph Ma-T'Ien-Chounn,
St. Mary Nan,
St. Mary Nan-Kouo-Cheu,
St. Anne Nan-Sinn-Cheu,
St. Anne Nan-Tsiao-Cheu,
St. Mary of Peace,
St. Mary of the Holy Birth,
St. Mary of Saint Justus,
St. Mary Adolfine,
St. Mary Amandina,
St. Martin Ou,
St. Peter Ou,
St. John-Baptist Ou-Man-T'Ang,
St. Lawrence Ouang,
St. Martha Ouang,
St. Paul Ou-Kiu-Nan,
St. Paul Ou-Wan-Chou,
St. John Ou-Wenn-Yinn,
St. Lawrence Pe-Man,
St. John Peter Neel,
St. Francis Regis Clet,
St. Joachim Royo Pérez,
St. Peter Sans I Jordá,
St. Thomas Sen-Ki-Kuo,
St. Francis Serrano Frías,
St. Gabriel Taurin Dufresse
St. Simon Tceng,
St. John Tchang,
St. John Tchang,
St. John Tchang,
St. Phillip Tchang,
St. Tchang-Haoi-Lou,
St. Theresa Tchang-Hene-Cheu,
St. Francis Tchang-Iun,
St. Peter Tchang-Pan-Nieu,
St. Mary Tchao,
St. Rose Tchao,
St. Mary Tchao-Kouo-Cheu,
St. John-Baptist Tchao-Ming,
St. Peter Tchao-Ming,
St. John Tchen,

St. Mary Tcheng-Su,
St. Rose Tch'Enn-Kai-Tsie,
St. Peter Tchou-Jeu-Sinn,
St. Mary Tchou-Ou-Cheu,
St. John-Baptist Tchou-Ou-Joei,
St. James Tciao-Tciuen-Sin,
St. Andrew Tien-K'Ing,
St. Magdalene Tou-Fong-Kiu,
St. Mary Tou-Tchao-Cheu,
St. Mary Tou-T'Ien-Cheu,
St. John of Trier,
St. Agnes Tsao Kouy,
St. Elizabeth Tsinn,
St. Simon Tsinn,
St. Mary Ts'I-U,
St. Barbara Ts'Oei-Lien-Cheu,
St. Patrick Tun,
St. Peter U-Ngan-Pan,
St. John Van,
St. Louis Versiglia,
St. Anne Wang,
St. Rose Wang-Hoei,
St. Joseph Wang-Jou-Mei,
St. John Wang-K'Oei-Sinn,
St. Joseph Wang-K'Oei-Tsu,
St. Mary Wang-Li-Cheu,
St. Peter Wang-Ol-Man,
St. Lucy Wang-Tcheng,
St. Peter Wang-Tsouo Long,
St. Lucy Wang-Wang-Cheu,
St. Lucy Y,
St. Joseph Yuang-Keng-Yinn,
St. Joseph Yuen,

Let us pray.

Almighty and Eternal God, in your infinite mercy and unfathomable wisdom, you deemed these one hundred and twenty lives to follow in the footsteps of your Divine Son - Christ Crucified. Bearing the crosses of abuse, slander, and scourging, they remained faithful and responded by their supreme act of selfless love - martyrdom. Through the intercession of the Blessed Chinese Martyrs, may they sustain and deliver us from all sufferings and free us from the worries and sorrows of this life. May we unite our prayers with theirs that the persecution of the followers of Christ, especially in China, cease. May the Blessed Virgin Mary, whose Immaculate Heart was pierced with a sword, intercede for us at the hour of our death and welcome us into your eternal glory.

Through the same Jesus Christ our Lord.
Amen.

About the Editor

Tim Drake is a Catholic convert from the Lutheran faith. He currently serves as executive editor of Catholic.net and features correspondent with the *National Catholic Register*.

His work has appeared in *Envoy Magazine, Lay Witness, Columbia, Faith and Family, Gilbert!, Celebrate Life*, and *Catholic World Report*. Tim and his wife, Mary, reside in Saint Cloud, Minnesota with their four children.

Printed in the United States
1421100004B/244